WAYNE COUNTY
INDIANA

WAYNE COUNTY
INDIANA

THE BATTLES FOR THE COURTHOUSE

CAROLYN LAFEVER

THE
History
PRESS

Published by The History Press
Charleston, SC 29403
www.historypress.net

First published 2010

Manufactured in the United States

ISBN 978.1.59629.882.8

Library of Congress Cataloging-in-Publication Data

Lafever, Carolyn.
Wayne County, Indiana : the battles for the courthouse / Carolyn Lafever.
p. cm.
Includes bibliographical references.
ISBN 978-1-59629-882-8
1. Wayne County (Ind.)--History. 2. Wayne County (Ind.)--History, Local. 3. Wayne County (Ind.)--Politics and government. 4. Courthouses--Indiana--Wayne County--History. 5. County government--Indiana--Wayne County--History. I. Title.
F532.W5L35 2010
977.2'63--dc22
2010013682

Notice: The information in this book is true and complete to the best of our knowledge. It is offered without guarantee on the part of the author or The History Press. The author and The History Press disclaim all liability in connection with the use of this book.

CONTENTS

ACKNOWLEDGEMENTS

Writers of the early Wayne County, Indiana history texts have left a wonderful legacy for later writers to use as resources. Without those, it would have been very difficult to piece together the story of Wayne County's "Battles for the Courthouse."

Collectors of newspaper articles, letters, diaries and photographs aided my search and verified information. I am grateful for their interest in preserving local history.

The person who helped me the most was my husband, Edward, who spent many hours preparing the pictures for this book. He transferred his photographs and my other pictures into our computer collection. These pictures should help bring the written words to life. Ed's photograph of the present courthouse was taken on an early winter morning just as the sun was illuminating the nearly 120-year-old gray limestone.

Jack Phelps has made drawings of all six courthouses. He is well known throughout the state for his excellent line drawings of historic buildings and bridges. His art has been exhibited at the Hoosier Salon, the Richmond Art Gallery and at many other places. Thank you, Jack, for helping us visualize the two courthouses, which were never photographed.

Wayne County Historical Museum director James Harlan located photographs and historical documents from the museum's extensive collection. We found missing pieces of history that benefited both the museum and my research.

The county libraries hold treasure-troves of information. Reference librarian Marilyn Knobbe and archivist Sue King assisted at the Morrison-Reeves Library in Richmond. Thomas Hamm, Earlham College Library archivist, contributed in the areas of Quaker and antislavery information. Librarians at the Centerville Center Township Public Library loaned rare books and pictures and opened their files for my inspection.

Gunty Atkins in the Wayne County surveyor's office, took time to find and refresh old maps and search through records to make the courthouse story more understandable.

A thank-you also goes to Franklin County historian Donald Dunaway, who filled in information, and photographer James Stevenson, who helped improve old pictures.

As the final draft was prepared, our three sons—David, Daniel and Douglas Lafever—came home to proofread and give suggestions for improvement. Their ideas and enthusiasm gave me an extra boost so that I could confidently finish this work.

It always amazes me how helpful people are by loaning whatever they have to aid my research. Many people encourage me, inquire about my progress on the book and look forward to it being published.

Thank you all. I hope you will enjoy reading the book as much as I have enjoyed writing it.

INTRODUCTION

Wayne County, Indiana, is located near the center of Indiana's east side, on the Ohio border. It has had three county seats and six courthouses. A courthouse, the most important building in the county, is the symbol of the "Seat of Justice." The story of the six courthouses built in Wayne County is one of conflicting community pride and stormy passions. This was the longest and most bitter battle in Indiana for locating a county seat—lasting more than sixty-two years!

The first struggle between Salisbury and Centerville caused considerable dissension. But it did not compare to the struggle of more than a half-century between Centerville and Richmond. The location of the county seat in Wayne County was a question not only of local politics but of Indiana politics as well. The election and appointment of county officials, circuit court judges, members of the legislature and even governors were affected by the regard for one town or the other. The struggle for the courthouse and county seat finally escalated into armed conflict.

Salisbury was the first county seat, Centerville the second and Richmond the third. There was a time when three of Wayne County's courthouses stood within a block of one another in Richmond, Indiana. A picture was taken in 1893 that shows both of the Richmond courthouses side by side. The first Richmond courthouse was built in 1873. It would soon after be torn down. The second Richmond courthouse was completed 1890–93. This new one—a huge, magnificent Bedford stone building—dwarfed the old brick courthouse.

Celebrated men: five heroes of the Northwest and Indiana Territories.

The first log courthouse, used from 1812 to 1817, was moved to Richmond in 1819. It was a two-story log structure first erected in the town of Salisbury in 1812. The builders of the town envisioned a bright future, and Salisbury was well on its way to becoming one of the most important towns in Indiana. But its prominence faded away when the county seat was moved to Centerville.

By 1818–20, two brick courthouses had been built, one in Salisbury and the other in Centerville. The log courthouse was no longer needed. It was sold and erected as a house on Front Street (now Fifth Street) in Richmond. In 1952, it was discovered under a covering of clapboard. Records proved that this had been the first Wayne County courthouse, still in its near original form.

The location of the first courthouse seemed unimportant, especially after five new courthouses had been built. But the log courthouse was to take on new life when Historic Centerville moved it to Centerville.

Stories about Wayne County's battles for the courthouse have been repeated many times, but as in most cases of recorded history, there is much more to be told.

CHAPTER 1

NORTHWEST TERRITORY AND THE FIRST WAYNE COUNTY

French missionaries and fur traders were the first Europeans to establish relations with the American Indians in the western territory of what would become the United States. By 1700, the French had established trading centers close to the Great Lakes, which were easily reached by waterways. Eventually, the French extended their territorial claims west to the Mississippi River and south to New Orleans, calling it New France. Spain owned the lands west and south of New France.

England also claimed territory in the New World by establishing thirteen colonies between 1607 and 1733. The colonies lay along the East Coast and extended as far west as Pennsylvania and south to the Florida border. It was inevitable that France and England would clash, as France wanted to keep the territory of New France and England wanted to expand to the south and west. The French and Indian War erupted in 1754. After fierce fighting for seven years and long negotiations, a treaty was signed in Paris in 1763. France surrendered its huge North American lands to England. At the same time, England gained the Spanish territory east of New Orleans.

The fighting forces of the French and Indian War were largely made up of British regulars and American militia. England trained many colonial military leaders, including George Washington. Those same experienced leaders later led the American War of Independence against England from 1776 to 1781. Other Revolutionary military heroes included George Rogers Clark and Anthony Wayne. The Treaty of Paris, signed in 1783, ended the

The Northwest Territory, 1787.

Revolutionary War and freed the colonies from England. This was the last barrier to the United States' complete sovereignty over its own lands.

At the end of the Revolutionary War, England ceded the area north of the Ohio River and west of the Appalachians to the United States, which became the Northwest Territory. But the presence of British outposts and continued hostilities with the Indians hampered efforts for American expansion. Several attempts were made by the loosely organized American forces to stop the harassment, but they were met with strong resistance.

General Arthur St. Clair was the first governor of the Northwest Territory. In 1788, he built his headquarters in Marietta, Ohio. St. Clair developed the first written laws for the territory. His mission was also to end the Indians' claims to Ohio lands and make the area safe for white settlers who were rapidly moving west.

St. Clair made many attempts to stop the hostilities, but his poor military leadership against the Indians in the Western Ohio Territory caused the U.S. Army to suffer a disastrous defeat at the Battle of the Wabash in 1791. Because of the huge loss of both military and civilian life, General Anthony Wayne replaced St. Clair as commander of the army in 1792.

Wayne's Army Victorious Over the Indians

President George Washington had recognized Anthony Wayne as a military genius when Wayne served in the Revolutionary War. Wayne was a veteran of Valley Forge and had led troops in other decisive battles of the Revolution. At the end of the war, Wayne was commissioned as a brigadier general. He was a born leader who was daring, brave and courageous and knew how to use his troops well. Wayne was the best choice to take over the ragtag militia of the Northwest Territory.

When Wayne took over in the Northwest Territory, he became general of the army. His mission was to build and command a new army. His headquarters was built near Cincinnati at Fort Washington. Wayne believed that earlier failures to defeat the Indians were due to poor training and discipline. The usual enlistment was for six months, but Wayne extended the time to keep the 1,600 regulars and 1,500 Kentucky militia ready for battle.

Peace negotiations with Indian leaders were underway by the federal government when Wayne became army commander. This allowed him time to train the newly named Legion of the United States, the first federal troops of the new republic. Wayne enforced new rules of discipline, including no liquor or womanizing (although not always completely successful in those areas). He trained an excellent cavalry and taught foot soldiers to load their guns while on the run. These battle skills were soon to rout the Indians and bring them to the bargaining table.

The new army moved north from Cincinnati, building a wide road called "Wayne's Trace." A series of forts was built between the Ohio and Maumee Rivers. The road and the forts kept the army well supplied. Among Wayne's officers was young William Henry Harrison, soon to be the first governor of the Indiana Territory and the ninth president of the United States.

In 1794, the army was in a position to confront Chief Blue Jacket and his allies. The conflict was called the Battle of Fallen Timbers; it was fought in a huge area of trees that had fallen due to a tornado. About one thousand Indians tried to conceal themselves among the downed trees, but they were greatly outnumbered. The battle took place about three miles southwest of the city of Maumee, Ohio, now a National Historic Site.

Wayne's army of more than 4,600 men won the battle with few casualties. This victory was one of the most important military achievements in U.S. history. It led to the Treaty of Greenville, signed on August 2, 1795. Migration into the Northwest Territory became relatively safe until hostilities broke out again in 1812.

The Battle of Fallen Timbers, 1794.

The Greenville Treaty was between the Untied States and a coalition of twelve Indian tribes known as the Western Confederacy. In exchange for goods valued at $20,000, the Indians turned over large parts of Ohio and areas extending west. This treaty gave the United States ultimate control of the Northwest Territory, which led to the statehood of Ohio and four other states.

General "Mad" Anthony Wayne was not without his critics. The nickname "Mad" was added by disgruntled troops who objected to the stern discipline. It stuck. The term was derogatory at first, but it came to signify his daring and courage, as well as his strong discipline and command of the troops. Wayne succeeded in defeating and negotiating with Americans Indians where other leaders had failed. It was because of his victories and leadership abilities that several counties in the midwestern United States honor him by bearing his name, including Wayne County, Indiana.

All the while Wayne was leading the army through the wilderness, he suffered greatly from gout. His condition was a disabling, swelling pain in the legs and feet, caused by malfunction of the kidneys. He continued to command the army and work on the treaty in spite of pain and swelling in his left leg. Many things were tried to help his illness, such as wrapping his leg in tight bandages. The doctors also bled him, thinking to relieve the swelling. But in 1796, while traveling to his home in Pennsylvania, Wayne died at age fifty-one of complications from gout. He is buried in Radnor, Pennsylvania.

Earlier, however, Wayne took over the armed forces, and St. Clair continued to serve as governor. A part of Governor St. Clair's duties was to form counties within the Northwest Territory. After Wayne's death, St. Clair set off another county in the territory and named it Wayne County, formed in 1796. It originally covered all of lower Michigan, northwestern Ohio, northern Indiana and a small portion of the Lake Michigan shoreline, including present-day Chicago. The seat of government was at Detroit.

CHAPTER 2
INDIANA TERRITORY

Indiana Territory was created in 1800 as part of the first division of the old Northwest Territory. In 1803, Ohio achieved statehood. Michigan Territory was split from Indiana Territory in 1805. Illinois Territory was formed in 1809, creating the present-day boundaries of Indiana. After these territories were formed, the Northwest Territory and the old Wayne County ceased to exist.

William Henry Harrison was appointed the first governor of the Indiana Territory. He had worked with the federal government to help set up the territory and was rewarded with the office. The first territorial legislature met in Vincennes on July 29, 1805. The legislature passed measures for taxing, organizing new courts, arranging licenses and other acts necessary for managing the large territory. There were no representatives from the present-day Wayne County since it had no permanent settlers and was part of Dearborn County, Indiana Territory.

The first land entries in this uninhabited part of Dearborn County were made by Peter Fleming and Joseph Wasson in the winter of 1804. The first settlers came to the present Wayne County in 1805. Richard Rue, George Holman and Thomas McCoy entered their claims at Cincinnati in 1804. They came with their families to the Elkhorn area, a few miles south of present-day Richmond. All three men had served in the Revolutionary War. Veterans of the war were offered land as a payment for their military service.

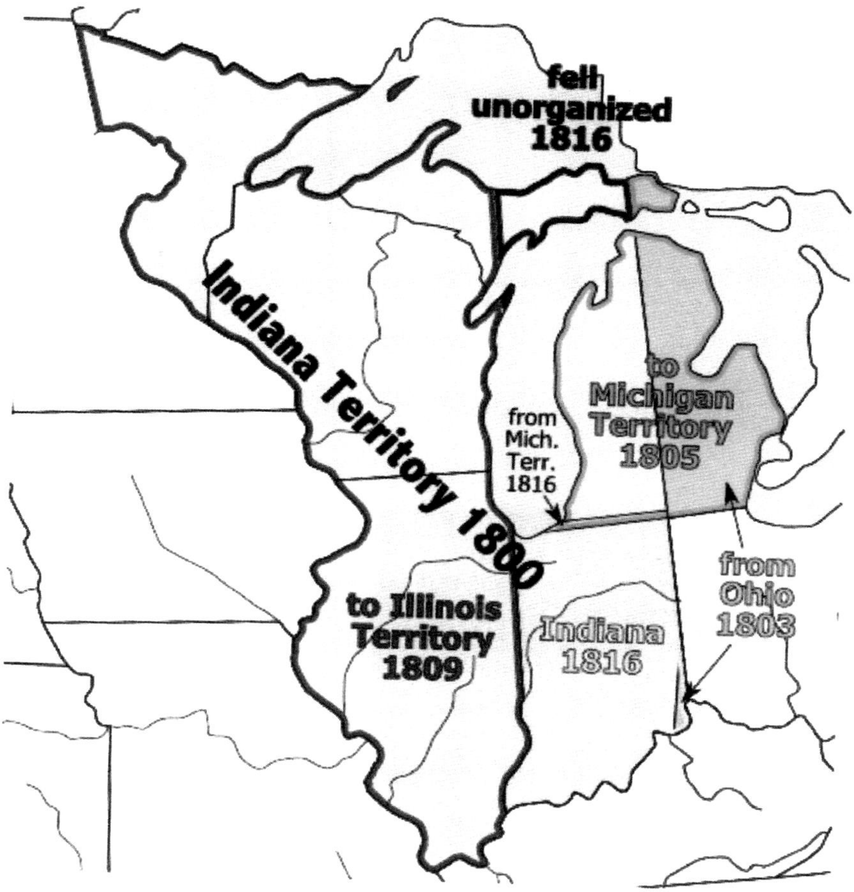

Indiana Territory 1800

The Indiana Territory, 1800.

Kentucky Cousins Captured by Indians

Richard Rue and George Holman were cousins. They served with George Rogers Clark, the Revolutionary War hero, when he captured Vincennes from the British in 1779. In 1781, while Rue and Holman were escorting

Evan Hinton with a load of barrels to Vincennes, they were captured by hostile Indians. All three were tortured and forced to run the gauntlet.

It was a custom of hostile Indians to force a prisoner to run the gauntlet, two lines of warriors armed with clubs and knives. All three men were forced to race for their lives while being severely beaten and struck. Evan Hinton managed to escape but was soon recaptured. He was burned at the stake.

Rue and Holman were separated and taken to two separate tribes by the Indians. For at least three years, they were held captive, suffering abuse and hardships. Rue eventually escaped with two fellow captives. Traveling by night and sleeping by day, they made their way back to Kentucky. Not long after Rue's

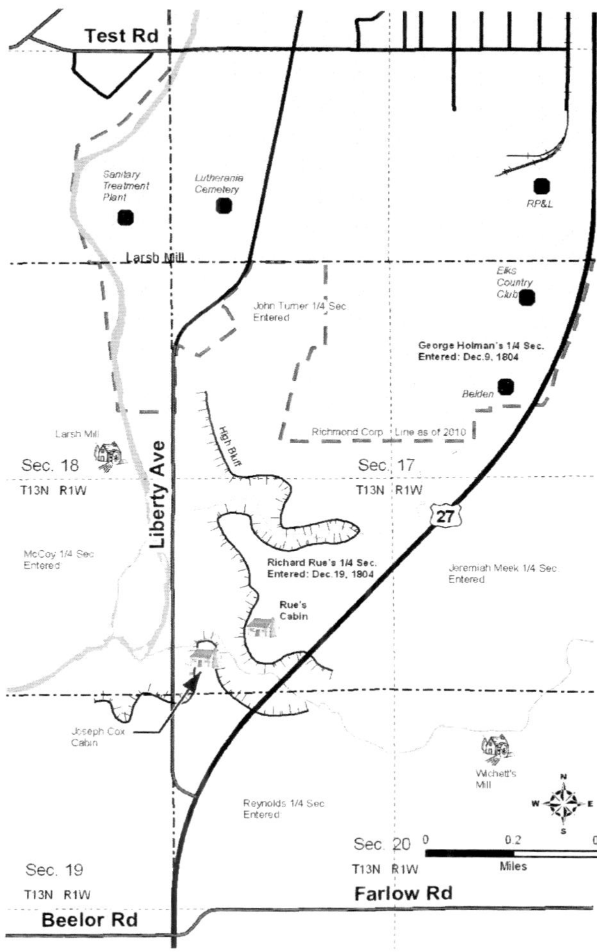

A map of Rue and Holman's home, location of the first settlers in Wayne County. *Map by Gunty Atkins.*

escape, Holman was allowed to travel home to collect a ransom from his uncle. After gaining their freedom from captivity, the two cousins settled in Kentucky.

A new law in Kentucky and a series of overlapping claims caused virtually all the early settlers to lose their land. Richard Rue and George Holman lost their property because it had not been correctly deeded to them. The cousins decided to move to the uninhabited northern part of Dearborn County, present-day Wayne County. Richard Rue had passed through the Whitewater Valley more than once. He knew that it would be a good place to settle. They recorded their deeds in Cincinnati and arrived in 1806.

The settlers who came from Kentucky were careful to enter their claims legally before establishing permanent homes. Others from the same area who had lost their lands moved into the same area as Rue and Holman had. The area south of Richmond became known as the Kentucky Settlement. Among those early settlers were the families of George Holman, Richard Rue, Joseph Cox, Thomas McCoy, Jeremiah Meek and John Turner.

QUAKERS ARRIVE

In 1806, Jeremiah Cox and John Smith purchased land and built homes in the area of the present courthouse in Richmond. Smith set up a trading post, the first business in the area. In 1806, David Hoover and four friends came into the county and explored the area near the west bank of the Whitewater River and north of Richmond. They visited with Rue and Holman and decided that this would be a good area to settle. They moved with their families in 1807.

Cox, Smith and Hoover were part of the Society of Friends, also called Quakers. By 1808, many more Quaker families had settled in the Whitewater Valley. Although the main attraction was the cheap land, fertile soil and abundant water, the Quakers also were coming to a place where slavery was not allowed. Both settlements of people in early Wayne County, the "Whitewater Quakers" and "Kentucky Baptists," had strong religious convictions against slavery. Their combined efforts against this injustice would have a strong influence in the politics of the Indiana Territory and the state of Indiana.

Not long after establishing his home, Richard Rue was appointed justice of the peace in Dearborn County by Governor Harrison. All appointments to political office were made by the governor until after a county was organized and ready for elections.

CHAPTER 3
A NEW WAYNE COUNTY

A new Wayne County was set off from the northern part of Dearborn County, which had been established in 1803. Wayne County's first boundaries encompassed the area known as the Gore. This triangular-shaped piece of land was the section of Indiana from the Ohio line west to the Greenville Treaty line. In 1809, Governor Harris bought land from the Indians, calling it the Twelve Mile Purchase. This added a strip of western land to Dearborn County. Boundaries continued to change as new counties were formed and more land was acquired from the Indians. More counties to the north and west were formed after Indiana became a state in 1816.

Wayne County, Indiana Territory, was formed in November 27, 1810 (effective January 1, 1811). Some writers date Wayne County's birth as 1810, and others date it 1811. The usual citation found in older histories and documents is the date it was formed by the Indiana Territory legislature.

Richard Rue was a member of the legislature that passed the act creating Wayne County. Although Governor Harrison had the power to make all appointments, he gave the people of the counties the privilege of electing their own officers.

Keeping slavery out of their new home was a concern for Wayne County's early settlers. The Kentucky Baptists came from a relatively free slave state because most landowners in Kentucky could not afford slaves. The first Whitewater Quakers were from the slave state of North Carolina. Both groups of settlers did not want to see slavery come into the Indiana Territory.

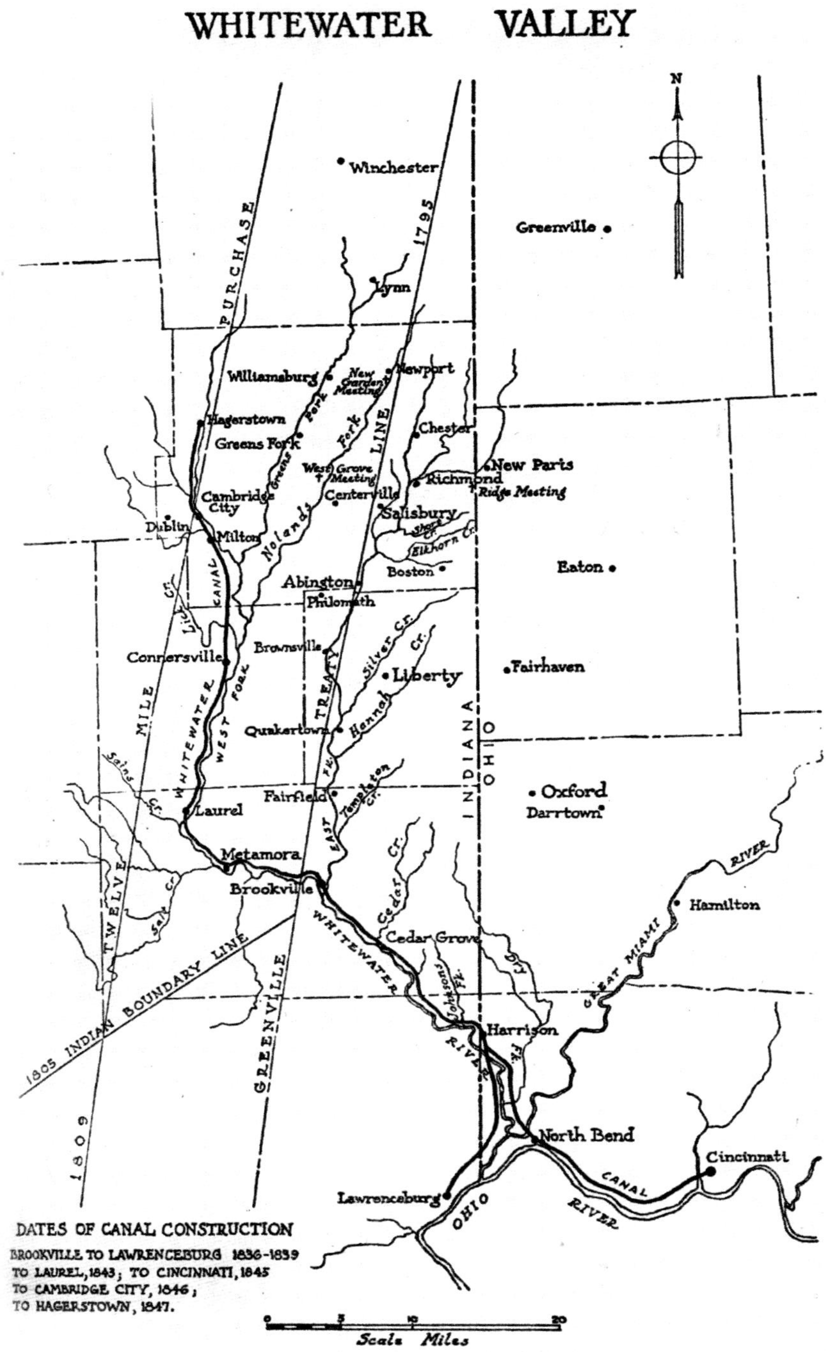

An 1850 map of Gore and Twelve Mile Purchase.

Taking care of community affairs was important to early settlers. Whenever there was business to transact, a settler's log cabin served as the meeting place. Notice for a meeting was often given at a logrolling, a community event during which people came to help build a cabin. In 1808, a meeting was called in the Whitewater area to choose a nominee for the election of a delegate to Congress from Dearborn County.

An attempt was being made to change the provision of the ordinance of 1787, which prohibited slavery in the Northwest Territory. The strong antislavery sentiments among the Whitewater settlers favored the election of a man who would represent their view. George Hunt was chosen as the conditional candidate.

Young Joseph Holman, one of the first eight to arrive and settle in the area, was chosen to confer with settlers on Clark's Grant. George Rogers Clark, Revolutionary War hero, was awarded this grant of 150,000 acres. This was given to Clark and his troops as a reward for winning battles against the British in the Northwest Territory.

Clark's Grant, Indiana Territory, was located across the Ohio River from Louisville. The grant was given by Virginia in 1782. Pioneers had settled in Clark's Grant, which was also a part of Dearborn County. Settlers came as early as 1784, the earliest settlements being Clarksville and Jeffersonville. In 1808, Jeffersonville became the site of the second federal land office for the Indiana Territory.

Joseph Holman made the long and difficult trip through the wilderness on horseback. His mission was to find out their views for selecting a representative for Dearborn County. George Hunt's name would be withdrawn if there were another suitable candidate. Jonathan Jennings, a foe of slavery, was the candidate selected to represent Dearborn by the people in Clark's Grant.

Indiana Territory governor Harrison, a native of Virginia, was on the side advocating for slavery. His impressive mansion, Grouseland, was built by slave labor, and he owned several slaves. Although the laws for the Northwest Territory prohibited slavery, Harrison wanted to see them changed. His choice for the Dearborn County candidate was Thomas Randolph.

The trip through the forest and wilderness kept Joseph Holman from returning home for several weeks. While Holman was traveling to Clark's Grant, the candidate Jonathan Jennings came to campaign in the Whitewater area.

Thomas Randolph, Governor Harrison's choice, was known for promoting slavery. He sent others to do his campaigning in the antislavery areas. Captain Vance and the Randolph delegation made it to the Whitewater Valley before Jennings. Vance was a stranger who might be able to fool the backwoods people into making him their candidate. He, in turn, would drop out in favor of Randolph. This would throw his votes to the candidate in favor of slavery.

The mission of the Randolph delegation was to "poison the minds of the people" against Jennings. He was characterized as "a beardless boy who couldn't find his way to Washington" and other choice insults.

When Joseph Holman arrived back home, he found a meeting in progress. Jonathan Jennings was in attendance. Vance's plan seemed to be working, and Jennings received a cold reception when he arrived in the Whitewater Valley. Holman told his story to his father and others privately, and after some consideration the local men approached Jennings. They showed him a circular that made serious accusations against him. Jennings was able to refute the charges and correct the lies. He was chosen to run against Randolph for Dearborn's representative to Congress.

Jonathan Jennings was elected to Congress but won by a margin of only twenty-six votes. He later became the first governor of Indiana in 1816. The efforts of Jennings and other like-minded legislators in Washington kept slavery out of the Indiana Territory.

GETTING DOWN TO BUSINESS

Wayne County was divided into two townships. County commissioners as we know them today did not serve in Indiana until it became a state in 1816. The county business and court-related affairs were conducted by three judges. An election was held in 1811, and Peter Fleming, Jeremiah Meek and Aaron Martin were the three elected. George Hunt was elected clerk and John Turner as sheriff.

Richard Rue, one of the first Wayne County residents, held many of the meetings at his cabin. He and David Hoover were appointed justices of the peace before the county was formed. They were appointed again in 1810 at the same time as the forming of Wayne County. The first local court of the county was held at Rue's cabin, and the county was organized on February 25, 1811.

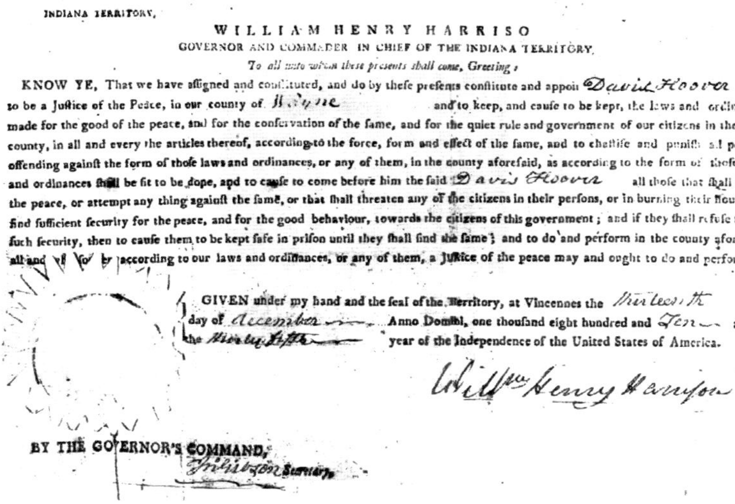

INDIANA TERRITORY,

WILLIAM HENRY HARRISO[N]

GOVERNOR AND COMMANDER IN CHIEF OF THE INDIANA TERRITORY,

To all unto whom these presents shall come, Greeting:

KNOW YE, That we have aſſigned and conſtituted, and do by theſe preſents conſtitute and appoint David Hoover to be a Juſtice of the Peace, in our county of Wayne and to keep, and cauſe to be kept, the laws and ordinances made for the good of the peace, and for the conſervation of the ſame, and for the quiet rule and government of our citizens in the ſaid county, in all and every the articles thereof, according to the force, form and effect of the ſame, and to chaſtiſe and puniſh all perſons offending againſt the form of thoſe laws and ordinances, or any of them, in the county aforeſaid, as according to the form of thoſe laws and ordinances ſhall be fit to be done, and to cauſe to come before him the ſaid David Hoover all thoſe that ſhall break the peace, or attempt any thing againſt the ſame, or that ſhall threaten any of the citizens in their perſons, or in burning their houſes, to find ſufficient ſecurity for the peace, and for the good behaviour, towards the citizens of this government; and if they ſhall refuſe to find ſuch ſecurity, then to cauſe them to be kept ſafe in priſon until they ſhall find the ſame; and to do and perform in the county aforeſaid, all and [illegible] according to our laws and ordinances, or any of them, a Juſtice of the peace may and ought to do and perform.

GIVEN under my hand and the ſeal of the Territory, at Vincennes the thirteenth day of December Anno Domini, one thouſand eight hundred and Ten and in the Thirty fifth year of the Independence of the United States of America.

Willm Henry Harrison

BY THE GOVERNOR'S COMMAND,

[illegible] Secretary.

David Hoover's commission as justice of the peace, 1810. *Courtesy of Wayne County Historical Museum.*

The first order of business for a county is to locate the seat of justice or county seat. The location of county government has great importance to any town or settlement. The courthouse is the symbol of the county and the center of political and social life. It is here that the principal county buildings—courthouse and jail—are located. Crime is prosecuted and marriages, births and deaths are recorded there. Even the architecture of the courthouse was important as a matter of county pride. Distances and directions were given and measured with the courthouse as the reference point. Being the "capital" of the county would bring business to the town. The county seat would naturally grow in importance and prosperity. It was not uncommon for several towns to battle bitterly for the position to gain the wealth and power.

The act of the territorial legislature to form Wayne County also appointed John Addington, George Holman and John Cox to select the best site for the county seat by May 1811. The law of the territorial legislature was to fix the county seat near the geographical center of the county.

Holman and Addington selected a place about three-fourths of a mile north of the present Centerville. Cox dissented because the land in the

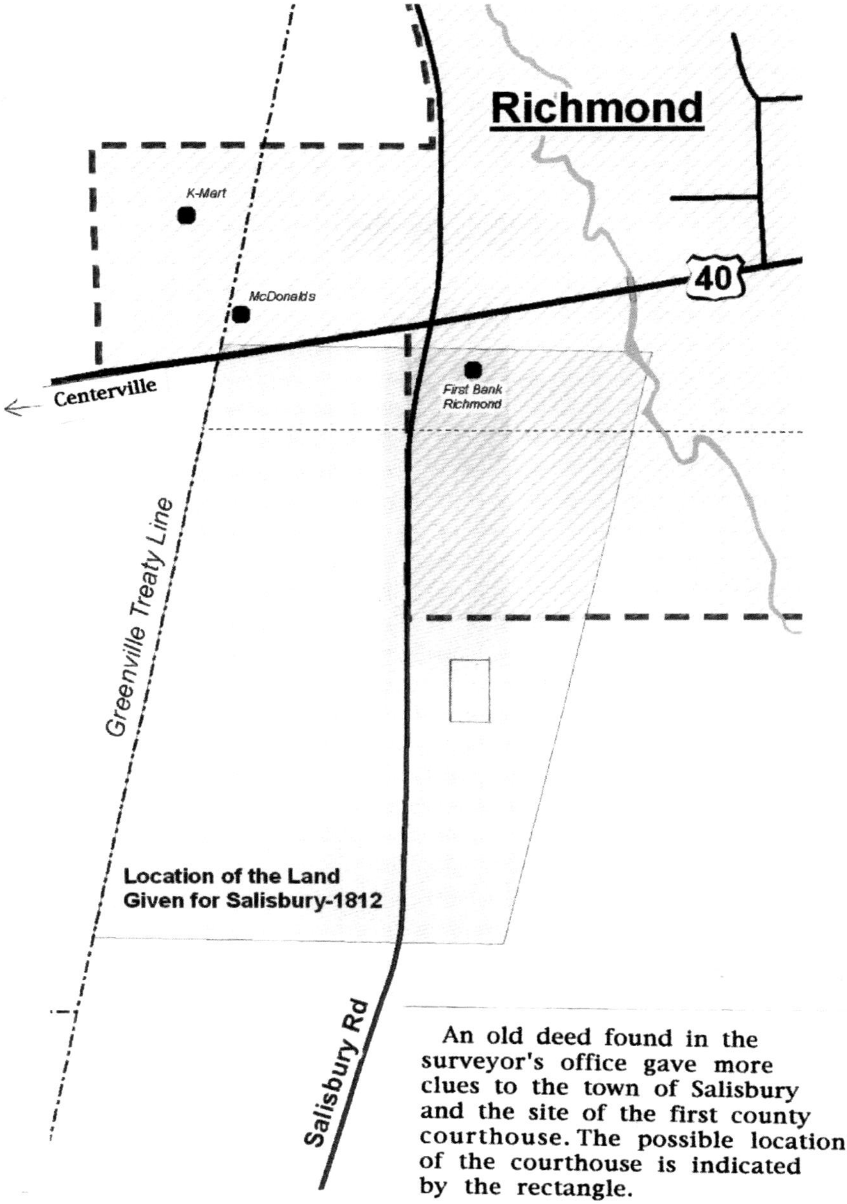

The site of Salisbury, located by the surveyor's office. *Map by Gunty Atkins.*

Twelve Mile Purchase where it was located was not offered for sale until later in the year. His argument was that they were not authorized to select land not yet sold by the federal government. Since the men could not agree, three other men were named to locate the county seat between what are now Centerville and Richmond.

The new decision of the county court was accepted: "That the permanent seat of justice is and shall be on the donation of Samuel Woods of 65 acres in the 13th township, range 3d, with a small reserve."

The court ordered "that the town in Wayne, or the seat of justice, shall be called Salisbury." Samuel Woods, Smith Hunt and James Brown were appointed trustees to lay off lots in the town to prepare them for sale. The court continued to be held at the house of Richard Rue, Esq., until a courthouse was built.

People who preferred a more central location denounced the action by the court. An informal vote was taken to get a sense of how the residents of Wayne County felt as to the legality of the court's decision. There were more opposed to the Salisbury location than those in favor, but the decision held. The location at Salisbury was confirmed by the fall session of the Indiana Territory legislature in November 1811.

A temporary log courthouse was ordered immediately. The contract was given to William Commons and paid for in June 1912. The initial cost was $229.99. Samuel Woods formally presented the deed to the land to the county on April 24, 1812. This date would indicate that Woods had not made the site available to the county until the spring of 1812.

There are writers of Wayne County history who quote sources that indicate that the log courthouse was constructed and in limited use in the fall of 1811. If there were more Wayne County records for 1811 that might have shed more light on this, they disappeared long ago. The sources quoted may have been passed along only as oral history. This information was not given in the 1872 or the 1884 Wayne County histories. However, it was printed more than one hundred years later in the 1912 *Memoirs of Wayne County*.

With the confirmation of Salisbury's claim coming in the winter, it is doubtful that much work had been done toward building a courthouse. It is more likely that the large logs were cut and prepared during the winter. The building could be put up quickly in the spring and early summer.

A simple log house can be built quickly by a few men. Timber was plentiful in the dense forests of the Whitewater Valley. The first courthouse, however,

The log courthouse at the Wayne County Fairgrounds location, 1954. *Courtesy of the author.*

was a well-constructed building of huge hewn logs, two stories high, with a large fireplace. It was thirty-one feet long and approximately twenty-seven feet wide. According to *Indiana Courthouses of the Nineteenth Century*, this type of construction required considerable skill and numerous tools.

A log jail and estray pen were built near the courthouse soon after. The log jail was probably built as temporary housing for offenders of the law. It had only two rooms and lacked amenities for long-term jail sentences. The estray pen, an outdoor fenced area, was used to hold stray animals that roamed around. They were held until their owners claimed them and paid a fine. If not claimed in due time, they could be sold.

All county business before 1812 was conducted at Rue's cabin, including any criminal offenses. Since there was no jail in the county until 1812, creative solutions were needed to hand out punishment to the guilty offenders. In Henry Fox's 1912 *Memoirs of Wayne County*, a story is quoted as told by Squire John Cox. The court at Rue's cabin was in session when a witness was convicted of contempt of court. He was ordered to have his neck be put under the corner of a rail fence. The fellow was strong, though, and threw off the weight of the fence. Judge Cox ordered that the culprit be put under the fence again, but this time three men sat on the fence until the punishment was over.

Squirrels, Earthquakes and War

The new settlers in Wayne County suffered a series of setbacks from nature as early as 1807. A horde of gray and black squirrels came through from north to south. They damaged the crops, eating everything in sight. They rushed on their way, not even stopping at the Ohio River, where many of them perished trying to swim across. Ohio offered a bounty on squirrel pelts and spent hundreds trying to rid the state of the pests.

Another series of hardships followed in the spring of 1811. Extensive floods covered the banks of many waterways and the Whitewater River. The wetlands and newly cleared fields were slow to dry out, and crops were planted late in the year.

The county seat question had barely been settled in late 1811 when a series of earthquakes shook the area. Between December 26, 1811, and late April 1812, catastrophic damage occurred throughout the Mississippi Valley.

An old print of Salisbury.

The first earthquake was centered in New Madrid, Missouri, and was felt as far away as Canada, Mexico, Boston and New Orleans. It was estimated years later to have been a 7.5 on the Richter scale, the largest ever in the United States. Towns were destroyed, buildings leveled and the courses of lakes and rivers disrupted. More than two thousand aftershocks, many of them as disastrous as the first, continued to shake for nearly five months.

The area around Brookville, a few miles south of Richmond, was sparsely populated in 1811. The community felt the strong earthquakes and people were frightened. The fledgling Baptist church congregation, after much prayer and consideration, decided that it was a divine warning and that they should build a church. Little Cedar Baptist Church was the result. This is considered to be the oldest church in Indiana that is still sited on its original foundation. The building was restored in 1955 and is owned by the Franklin County Historical Society in Brookville.

Wayne County had few residents at the time, with only small log cabins on their farms. There were no reports of damage resulting from the earthquakes. The courthouse was not built until after the quakes stopped. However, in 1881, a group of pioneers at the Old Settlers' Picnic told how iron cooking utensils rattled against the stone fireplaces during the time of the earthquakes.

WAR OF 1812

In June 1811, hostilities and war came to the Indiana Territory when the British and their Indian allies captured Detroit. The British owned Canada but had never really given up their desire to regain ownership of western lands in America. Governor William Henry Harrison continued to negotiate land purchases from the Indians. Tecumseh and his brother "The Prophet" refused to abide by the agreements. They began a campaign to unite the Indian tribes of the Midwest to take back their lost lands. The news of the British victory in Detroit gave the Indian leaders encouragement to take up arms again. Harrison immediately took command of the army and marched against Tecumseh. He won a decisive defeat against the Indians at the Battle of Tippecanoe near Lafayette in November 1811.

Shortly after Harrison's victory at Tippecanoe, the territorial legislature met for the fall session in Vincennes, November 11–19, 1811. All of the important business of the counties was decided by the Territorial General Assembly. Richard Rue was the representative to the territorial legislature that November.

The relative safety enjoyed by the settlers was shaken by the possible threat of further Indian hostilities. It was the view of some that the Indians were encouraged to wage war for the benefit of greed and British desire to keep the fur trade. War was declared between the United States and the British empire in 1812.

County Seat Battle Begins

The battle for moving the county seat had already begun. Opponents of Salisbury urged their representatives to petition for changing the county seat to a more central location even before Salisbury was established by act of the legislature.

The bill by James Dill of Dearborn County to establish Salisbury as the seat of Wayne County was introduced on November 14, 1811. That same day, he also introduced a petition of the citizens of Wayne County to impeach Peter Fleming, Aaron Martin and Jeremiah Meek, the judges who had agreed to make Salisbury the seat. Another motion was made "to

Dr. David Sackett and wife, residents of Salisbury. *Courtesy of Wayne County Historical Museum.*

throw the said petition under the Table upon the question being taken it was carried in the negative." A tied vote was taken to refer the impeachment matter to a committee. The matter was tabled and later dismissed as lacking evidence against the judges.

Governor Harrison signed the act to make Salisbury the county seat. In the same session, it was allowed to make Quakers and Shakers pay an annual fine if they refused duty in the militia. Rules for platting a town were spelled out. The various acts took effect in 1812.

David Hoover, one of Wayne County's first settlers, tells in his memoirs the story of four young Quakers who refused the draft call for the war in the

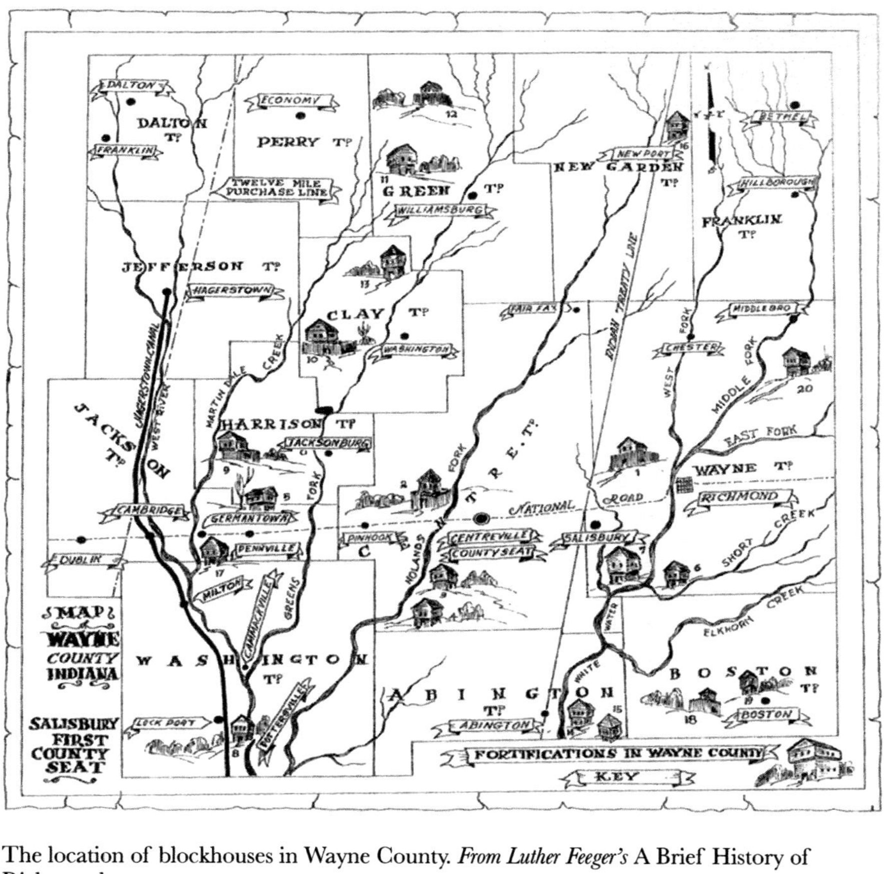

The location of blockhouses in Wayne County. *From Luther Feeger's* A Brief History of Richmond.

winter of 1812. Quaker faith did not allow them to take up arms against others, and they were harassed because they refused to take part in military duty. If they refused to serve in the militia, their property was confiscated or they paid heavy fines.

The weather was bitterly cold when the young men were jailed. They were not allowed to have a fire until they would agree to serve in the militia. Dr. David F. Sackett, Wayne County's first physician, did not condone their suffering and handed them hot bricks, hot drinks and blankets through the grates. They were released after several days. Suits were brought against the arresting officers for false imprisonment. The young men were awarded damages, but in the opinion of David Hoover, their awards came from moneys extorted from other Quakers.

Governor Harrison came to Salisbury in late 1812 to warn the citizens of the brewing hostilities of the Indians and to prepare the militia for battle. According to an account by Mrs. W.W. Gaar, a descendant of Jacob Meek, one of the first settlers, "Thirty or forty Indians were present when Harrison reviewed the militia." This gathering of Indians was reported to be the last large group anyone saw in Wayne County.

Immediately, several log houses were reinforced or made into blockhouses. A few small walled forts were built, enclosing the area around a blockhouse with a strong wooden fence. Among houses fortified in the county was the home of Isaac Julian. Joseph Holman, son of George Holman, had built a home near the soon-to-be-platted Centerville. He reported years later that he had built a blockhouse on his farm.

A two-story log cabin could be converted into a blockhouse by removing the top floor. The second story would be reconstructed with logs two or three feet longer, making an overhang all around the house. This would make the blockhouse tall enough to see over the top of a high fence. The men protecting the house or fort could fire down on any attackers.

Neighbors or family members moved together for protection. A few families temporarily left the territory. The fear was great, although there were no battles fought in the county and only a few incidents with Indians.

Because of Harrison's successful campaign at Tippecanoe earlier in 1811, Indiana experienced much less of the combat. Harrison resigned as governor in 1812. John Gibson served from 1812 to 1813. Thomas Posey was the last Indiana Territory governor, from 1812 to 1816. Harrison continued to lead his militia forces until the war was over. The major battles between the colonists and the British took place in the eastern United States. Parts of the country suffered greatly. The British entered and burned Washington City on April 24, 1814.

Oliver Hazard Perry defeated the British at the Battle of Lake Erie on September 10, 1813. This was a decisive battle for the American army in the Midwest, after which the British squadron surrendered. Perry sent word to William Henry Harrison in this famous message scrawled on the back of an old envelope:

> *Dear General:*
> *We have met the enemy and they are ours. Two ships, two brigs, one schooner and one sloop.*
> *Yours with great respect and esteem,*
> *O.H. Perry*

The British unsuccessfully bombarded Fort McHenry on September 13, 1814, during the Battle of Baltimore. Francis Scott Key wrote his famous poem while standing on the deck of a ship and watching the large American flag waving over Fort McHenry. The words were set to music, and it became our national anthem, "The Star-Spangled Banner." The War of 1812 ended with the Treaty of Ghent on February 16, 1815.

THE COUNTY GETS BACK TO BUSINESS

The political business of Wayne County accomplished little during its first months, perhaps because of the war scare. The first recorded minutes of the circuit court conducting the county business was dated June 1811. The next records in the commissioners' books are dated June 1812. The first business licenses issued in Salisbury began in September 1813.

Although Salisbury had a slow start after becoming the county seat, business soon began to pick up, and the commissioners' records show licenses recorded for the purpose of selling merchandise or setting up a tavern. Taverns were sometimes respites for travelers but more often the place for locals to imbibe strong drink. These establishments sold food and liquor, and some had sleeping rooms for travelers.

The founders of Salisbury had high hopes for its prosperity. The original plat map disappeared many years ago from the courthouse. Several historical writers have related that, on the back of the original plat map, this statement was found in the handwriting of George Hunt, county clerk and recorder:

> *The town of Salisbury stands on a beautiful site on the waters of Clear Creek W.C.I.T.* [Wayne County Indiana Territory] *in a fine neighborhood, envisioned by rich land, etc. No better water in the world—the air salubrious—and its elevated situation commands an extensive and beautiful prospect, and we flatter ourselves, that in a few years Art with her sister Industry will convert it from a forest to a flourishing inland town. Several gentlemen of property, have purchased lots, both in the merchantile and mechanical line, which will greatly enhance its value.*

Life was not easy for Wayne County settlers. They had to hunt wild game until their stock and crops produced enough to eat. Supplies came in from distant settlements in Ohio by packhorse.

Charles Coffin lived in Wayne County from 1824 to 1833. According to his memoirs, "The first settlers lived in a rough and simple way, mostly upon Hog and Hominy and upon cornbread, as corn was raised the first thing after the clearing of a piece of ground."

Wayne County was covered with dense forests. There were no roads, and settlers had to travel on dirt trails made by the Indians or animals. Streams had no bridges. Trees had to be hand-cut to let a narrow wagon through. People walked; few rode horses. The trails were muddy and it was slow going. It was not until after Indiana became a state that Wayne County began to appoint men to oversee the buildings of roads and cart ways. The first roads that were opened led primarily to Salisbury, coming from the Richmond and Centerville areas. By 1815, Salisbury was becoming one of the most important towns in the territory.

The Conflict Begins

Centerville was laid out in 1814 by its first trustees—Isaac Julian, Joseph Holman and William Harvey. At the time of its platting, a public square was set aside. Foes of Salisbury were thinking ahead to a time when the county seat would be located in the center of the county, as the law stated.

James Brown, who helped lay out Salisbury, was elected a representative from Wayne County to the Indiana territorial legislature in February 1813. Brown presented his credentials to the territorial legislature for certification. Immediately, a written document was introduced to the credentials committee containing evidence to show that James Brown was not legally elected. He had won by one vote against Joseph Holman.

Elijah Fisher of Wayne County also gave a notice affirming the opposing document. The petition was taken under advisement. A couple of days later, the committee reported that it had carefully examined the evidence and saw no sufficient grounds to set aside the election of Brown. The Salisbury forces had won again.

In 1814, James Brown died before the end of the legislative session. Joseph Holman, who ran against him, was appointed to take his place for the legislative session on December 4, 1815. The first day of the session, Holman petitioned the House that "sundry inhabitants of the county of Wayne [were] praying [for] a removal of the seat of Justice of said county together with divers remonstrances against the same."

As compensation for trying to move the county seat, Holman introduced bills to incorporate and regulate both Salisbury and Centerville. The bills passed. The act for changing the county seat of Wayne County was brought before the House for a vote on December 23, but the committee chose to postpone it indefinitely. Holman was given permission to take a leave of absence for the balance of the session.

Salisbury loyalists were not letting up in their efforts to keep the county seat. They planned a permanent courthouse to replace the temporary log building. On October 12, 1816, an order was issued from the commissioners to pay $896.94½ for the building of a new brick courthouse in Salisbury.

CHAPTER 4

INDIANA BECOMES A STATE

Congress passed a bill on April 19, 1816, making Indiana a state. The act provided for forty-three delegates to meet at a convention to decide whether to form a state government, and if so, they could create a state constitution. Joseph Holman was elected from Wayne County and was the youngest member of the delegation. He was also the youngest member in the Indiana state legislature who helped write the constitution. The other Wayne County delegates were Patrick Beard, Jeremiah Cox and Hugh Cull. The convention met in June, and the original Indiana constitution was completed on June 19, 1816.

Joseph Holman lived near Centerville and was an advocate for moving the county seat from Salisbury to Centerville. Holman was one of the early settlers in Center Township after he married and purchased his own land. He helped lay out the town of Centerville in 1814 and was one of its first trustees. He had a vested interest in seeing it thrive through becoming the county seat.

The next session of the Indiana legislature was held in December 1816. Holman campaigned again for moving the county seat to Centerville. This time he was successful, and an act was passed on December 21, 1816, authorizing the removal from Salisbury. The conditions laid down for the removal were that the citizens of Centerville would provide public buildings equal in "value and convenience" to those already in Salisbury. In other words, the Centerville public buildings should be as much like the ones in Salisbury as possible. They were to be completed at no expense to the

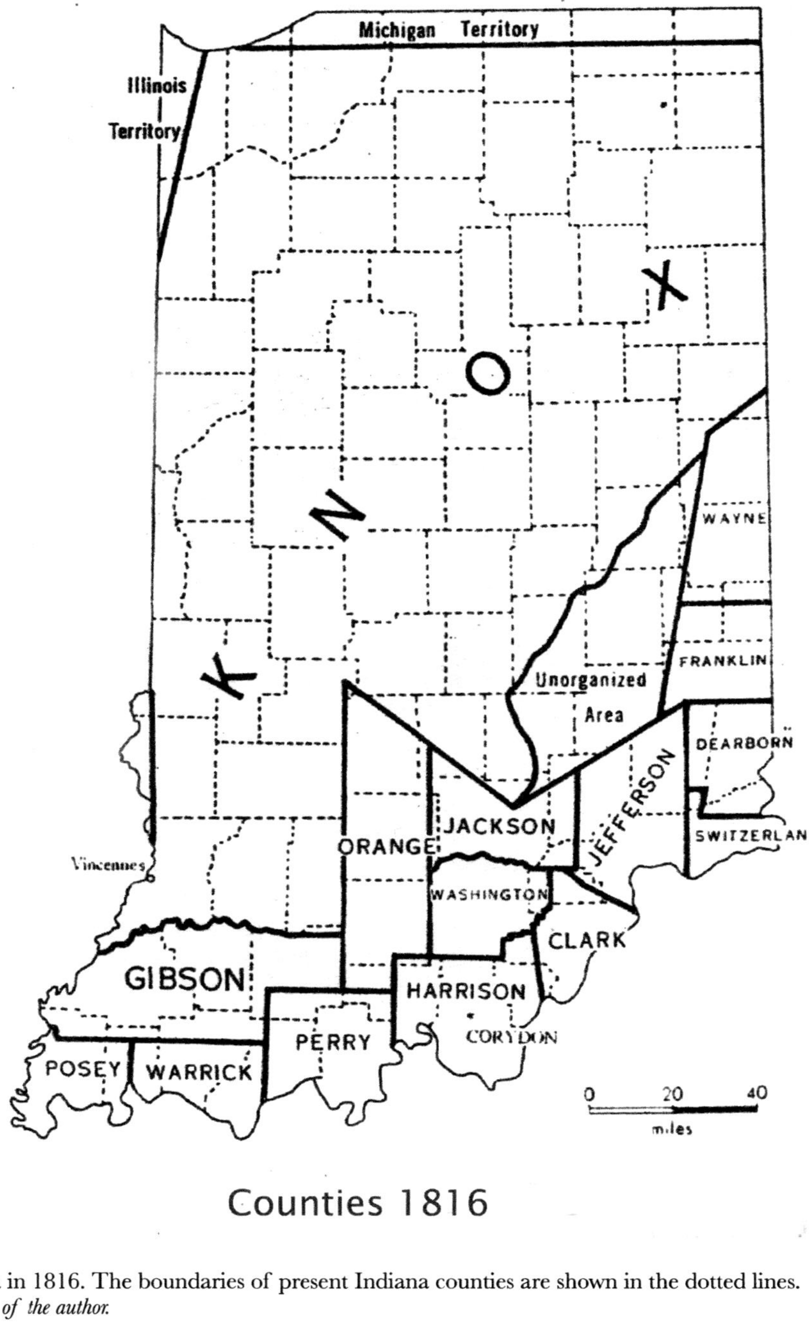

Indiana in 1816. The boundaries of present Indiana counties are shown in the dotted lines. *Courtesy of the author.*

Joseph Holman.

county. If Centerville failed to fulfill the conditions, Salisbury would remain the county seat. August 1, 1817, was named the day on which all public business would be moved to Centerville.

In February 1817, John Kibbey was appointed to "clear the old log courthouse, hang the doors and keep the same in repair." Three commissioners (or an appointed committee of three) were to "superintend the building of the Court House in the town of Salisbury with the same authority that they had by virtue of the appointment of the County aforesaid."

Salisbury was undaunted by the legislature and continued to build the new brick courthouse next to the log courthouse. A prolonged struggle between the two towns had begun.

Centerville Wins This Battle

The Indiana constitution provided for three commissioners, instead of judges, to oversee public business. The first record of elected commissioners in Wayne County is dated February 1817. Thomas J. Warman, James Odell and Thomas Beard produced their certificates of election and conducted the three-day session. The business was mostly setting up townships, appointing supervisors for opening roads, letting out business licenses, setting up elections for the townships and regulating other affairs.

A special meeting of the commissioners was called for July 21, 1817. Trustees of the town of Centerville came forward to present deeds, bonds and papers to the commissioners. They also produced a bond for $10,000 for the building of a courthouse in Centerville. The bond would be void if the buildings in the town of Centerville "were not completed equal in point of value and convenience according to the true intent and meaning of an act of the last general assembly." The trustees of Centerville had agreed to these terms laid down by the state legislature.

There was much anger and agitation between the citizens of Salisbury and Centerville. Six men from Centerville were assigned to examine and take down the description of the courthouse in Salisbury. They were to meet on August 23 at the courthouse.

The story told by early settlers is that the men from Centerville came to measure the new brick courthouse in Salisbury, but the people of Salisbury took up their guns to form a protective barrier around the public buildings.

A drawing of Salisbury courthouses. *Courtesy of Jack Phelps.*

A drawing of the Centerville courthouse. *Courtesy of Jack Phelps.*

The Centerville men were not allowed to go into the courthouse. They came as close as they dared and counted the bricks to get some idea of the size. Accurate measurements were needed to build the courthouse in Centerville just like the one in Salisbury. The men were kept from even getting close to the jail and estray pen, so they had to estimate those sizes.

There is no description of either the Salisbury or first Centerville brick courthouses. However, upon researching other Indiana courthouses of the period, many were built similar to the one built in Corydon. An artist's concept of both of these courthouses is of a square design, with two stories and a cupola bell tower. Later commissioners' records would show repairs to the cupola.

At this time, there were no known brickyards in the county. Bricks were made and fired by the builder on-site. Firing the bricks in an earthen oven caused their hardness to be uneven. The softer bricks were used on the inside and the hardest bricks on the outside of the wall. Hard brick is better able to take the harsh elements of weather. Two rows of bricks made for very thick, strong walls.

On February 9, 1817, according to commissioners' records, "David Hoover was to have the privilege of the house assigned for a Court House in the town of Centerville for the express purpose of holding his office in it without being detrimental to the holding of courts in the same." This was a temporary location for county courts to be held in Centerville.

In 1819, Edmond Dana, an early traveler in Indiana, reported in his *Geographical Sketches on the Western Country Designed for Emigrants and Settler*:

> *Salisbury, formerly the county seat of Wayne, situated on a head branch of Whitewater river, is but two miles eastwardly of Centreville, the latter place consisting on a few cabbins in the woods, where the courts are not holden… on application to the legislature, commissioners have been appointed to designate the spot for a permanent establishment. Two expensive brick court houses have already been erected, one at Salisbury and the other at Centreville, not more than two miles apart.*

SALISBURY: ONE LAST TRY

Advocates for Salisbury were very upset about the county seat move. A petition was circulated and pledges were made to help pay for the completion of the Salisbury brick courthouse on June 25, 1818. The handwritten petition reads:

> *To Whom It May Concern*
> *The undersigned citizens of Wayne County and State of Indiana Viewing the dissatisfaction and contentions which prevails among the Citizens of said County respecting the permanent seat of Justice of the same, And after taking the Subject under mature consideration they conceive that something further was necessary to be done in order to have the dispute decided. And as the undersigned feel a disposition to have the said differences amicably decided they feel willing to announce to their fellow Citizens that they expect to address the next legislature on the subject praying them to appoint disinterested men to decide for them where the permanent seat of Justice shall be. They will further add that should the commissioners appointed Establish the seat of Justice for said County in the Town of Salisbury that they will defray all expenses that are at this time due from said County towards building the public Court House in said town of Salisbury. And in order to carry this last clause compleately into effect we whose names are*

> *hereunto subscribed each for himself his heirs Executors and Administrators do promise to pay or cause to be paid to the board of commissioners of said County or to such other person or persons as shall or may be appointed to supertend the collections & appropriation of the same the sum of money to our names be respectively annexed to be appropriated to the express purpose of defraying the expense in finishing the Court house in the town of Salisbury and no other use intent on or purpose whatever. The one half of said subscription to be paid in two months after the same is permanently established in the Town of Salisbury and the other in six months after the first payment. Witness our hand & seal this 25th day of June 1818.*

Thirty-seven men pledged from $5 to $300, totaling $2,600, to help keep the county seat in Salisbury. Two men from outside the county—John

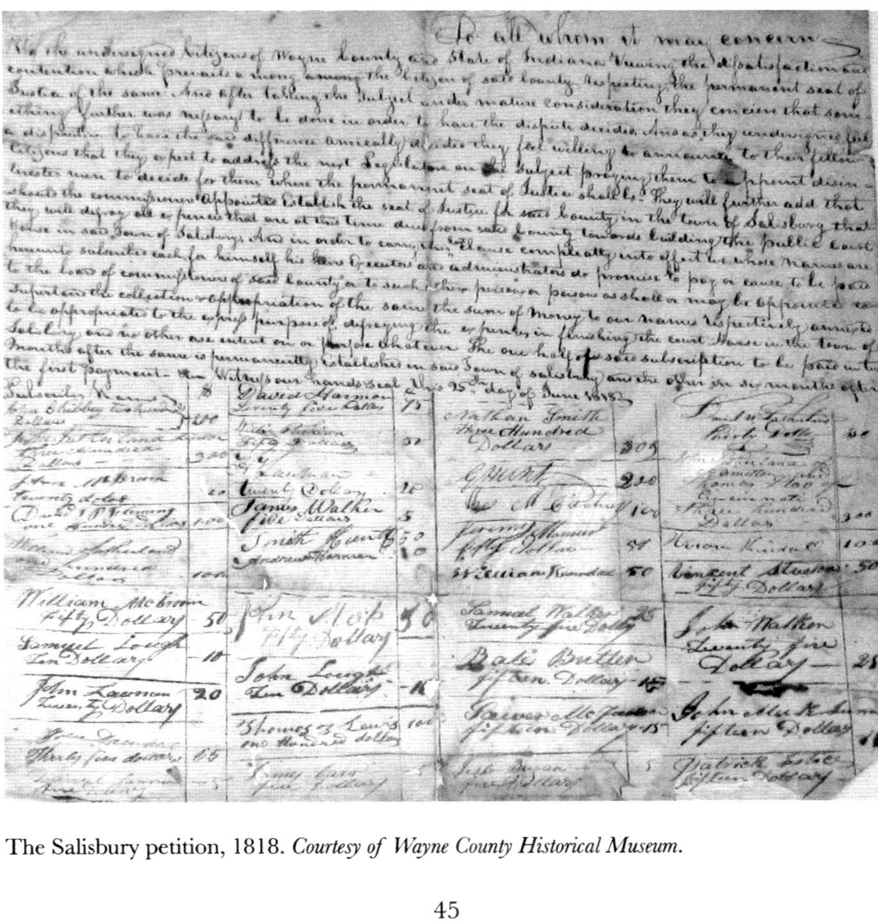

To all whom it may concern

The Salisbury petition, 1818. *Courtesy of Wayne County Historical Museum.*

Southerland of Hamilton, Ohio, and Thomas L. of Cincinnati—together pledged $300. It is likely that they had business interests in Salisbury and did not want to see them jeopardized.

The log courthouse was no longer needed, and plans were made to sell it and other public property at auction in Salisbury on July 5, 1818. Commissioner Thomas Warman objected to the sale and left his seat. There is no record of what was paid for the log building. It was purchased and moved to Richmond, which was still a very young town. It was customary to move log buildings, for they were relatively easy to take down and rebuild. This was an inexpensive way to reuse valuable materials.

The next commissioners' meeting was held in August 1818. Payment of $1,000 was made to Robert Kendall for the fourth installment on the Salisbury brick courthouse. This brought the total building costs to $4,000. Kendall was to submit the courthouse to the inspection of Abraham Laure and Peter Johnson as to the workmanship and completion of the building. They employed four other men to help with the actual inspection.

On February 1819, the county commissioners met in the brick courthouse in Salisbury. On February 11, the board of commissioners ordered a commissioner's seal to be made for their use. It was "a plow and sheaf of wheat engraved on the same with such other letters and devices on the same as may be thought appropriate," according to commissioners' records.

Centerville went forward with plans for a brick courthouse. During the May 19, 1819 session, William Sumner came to the commissioners with a deed for the public square in the town of Centerville for the permanent seat of justice. After deliberating for a time, "The Commissioners consider that under the law, the decision of the Circuit Court and the way in which said Deed appears to be executed they are not authorized to receive said Deed."

The commissioners' books record no comments, but rejecting this deed no doubt would have angered the Centerville advocates and made them more determined to be victorious over Salisbury.

In August 1819, Isaac Julian took Beale Butler's place as a commissioner with Thomas Warman and Enos Grave. Isaac Julian brought up the first action of the board. Insisting that the board move to Centerville, he quoted the act of the state legislature of December 21, 1816, which removed the seat of justice from Salisbury to Centerville. He quoted the conditions that were set down for the Centerville trustees. The trustees had complied with all of the conditions. Another act by the state legislature on January 28,

1818, declared that the courts would be held in Centerville. A decision by the court, possibly a district court, held that courts would take place in Centerville until altered by law. It appears that the case was confirmed by an outside court, as well as the state legislature.

A local judge, Watt, at the same meeting came down hard on the clerk of the county. He strongly advised him against moving the clerk's office back to Salisbury from Centerville since it had already been moved there by an earlier order. But the board overruled Watt's motion to keep the clerk's office in Centerville. It also would not accept Julian's credentials to take his seat at Salisbury. There are no comments as to how Julian took this insult, but he did not take his seat as a commissioner. The rest of that year, the commissioners' records are signed only by Warman and Grave. Julian's signature was conspicuously missing.

At the November meetings, Isaac Julian was still absent. His name appears as a viewer of a public road for which he was paid. Later, the commissioners must have reflected on their decision, or perhaps there was a compromise with Julian.

The first session of 1820 began on February 14. On the second day, Isaac Julian appeared and took his seat as commissioner. At this session, David Hoover was paid $65.37 for the purchase of a stove for the courthouse. He was also charged with selecting someone to make repairs to the courthouse in Salisbury.

In August 1820, a newly elected Wayne County commissioner, Benjamin Harris, produced his certificate of election. Isaac Julian and Harris introduced a motion for the commissioners to adjourn to Centerville and meet there at two o'clock in the afternoon. Enos Grave vehemently protested. He formally submitted this protest:

> *That he* [Enos Grave] *does conceive in the strongest term that the first section of the law authorizing the removal of the seat of Justice from Salisbury to Centerville approved December 21, 1816 has not been complied with and by reference to the proviso in the fourth section of said Act it does clearly and conclusively appear that in such as the provisions of that act have not been complied with, the Seat of Justice for the County of Wayne is to all intents and purpose in the Town of Salisbury. He further represents that he is strongly confirmed on this opinion by the decision of the Circuit Court of Wayne County after the question had been fairly and fully*

> *argued and that a decision from such a source is entitled to considerable right, and also that the act of 1820 appointing disinterested men clearly infer that the Seat of Justice was in dispute which certainly was the understanding. Isaac Julian, one of the Commissioners when he took his seat in the Town of Salisbury and publicly stated that he considered that the act appointing disinterested men had obviated the difficulty he felt himself under in sitting in Salisbury from these considerations he does protest against the decision adjourning the Commissioners Court to Centerville.*

Enos Grave

The board met at Centerville anyway, but Enos Grave refused to serve for that session. He drew up the protest and entered it in the records outside of a meeting. Julian and Harris signed the record book, but according to them, they were only signing for the proceedings and not accepting Grave's protest.

William Sumner and his wife again produced a deed for the public square in the town of Centerville. The board of commissioners accepted the deed and agreed that all conditions had been met for the removal of the county seat.

Enos Grave came back to the board at the November 1820 meeting. Sometimes only two of the commissioners attended the meetings. Emotions must have cooled, since the records show that most of the commissioners' business was appointing and hearing from road supervisors and reports of routine affairs. The county clerk was given a key so that he could move his office into the northwest room in the upper story of the Centerville courthouse.

CHAPTER 5

CENTERVILLE

The Notable Town of the County

Centerville began growing rapidly. The mail route from the East passed through Centerville on its way to Indianapolis. This was an important distinction as it was one of the collection points for people to send or receive mail. Business moved from Salisbury to Centerville. Lawyers and county officials moved their private offices into the town. As early as 1817, *The Emigrants Directory* noted, "Salisbury…lies 30 miles north of Brookville, contains about thirty-five houses, two stores and two taverns. It is at present the Seat of Justice for Wayne County, but Centerville, a near village being more central threatens to become its competitor for that privilege."

In May 1821, a new jail to replace the temporary one was ordered for Centerville. The lowest bid was Thomas Commons for the sum of $2,000, with the work to be completed in August 1822. A new commissioner, John Jones, took the place of Enos Grave in August 1821.

The squabble over the county seat issue caused rifts in some of the leading families. David Hoover served as clerk of the court, and he was a Salisbury advocate. Isaac Julian, husband of Hoover's sister, was a Centerville man and a founder of the town. Their disagreement created a family estrangement, for both were "fixed in their thinking," according to a book by George W. Julian's daughter.

Isaac Julian was elected by the Whig Party to the Indiana legislature in 1822. It was held in Corydon, which was the capital of the state. Julian had become involved in signing notes for a friend on the eve of a financial panic. After completing the term in the legislature, he sold his farm to

An image of Isaac Julian's home before it was a blockhouse.

pay off the notes and prepared to move. No doubt his financial problems, the estrangement in the family and the continued fighting between the Centerville and Salisbury factions led to his desire to relocate to a new area.

Isaac Julian chose a location for his home about eight miles south of the present city of Lafayette. He spent some time at the site, preparing it and building a cabin. During the time he was away, he became ill. Julian came back for his family. He traveled to his new cabin with his wife, Rebecca, and his six children in a covered wagon. When the family arrived, Isaac relapsed in his illness and died on December 12, 1823. The family was assisted by a kindly neighbor in returning to Wayne County. Henry Hoover, another of Rebecca Julian's brothers, welcomed them into his home until they could purchase a new place.

One of the Julians' six children was George Julian, born in 1817. He became a representative in the House of Congress and was an outspoken advocate for abolition of slavery. George's brothers, Isaac and Jacob Julian, also became prominent citizens of Centerville.

In 1816, another town was platted in Wayne County by the name of Richmond. The town as platted included the settlement of Smithville, the location of John Smith's trading post. The town was surveyed, and lots were laid out by David Hoover for John Smith. In 1818, Jeremiah Cox made an addition. A primitive road was already in place that would become Richmond's Main Street. By 1818, there was about two hundred people living in Richmond, and it was growing rapidly.

Capital Punishment in the Early Courts

The courts and justices of the peace served important roles in county business. Most of the crimes that brought in fines were profane swearing, assault and battery, affray (fighting between two or more people) and Sabbath breaking. It was rare for the fines to be more than one dollar. On at least two occasions, a woman named Beverly Cary was fined fifty cents for assault and battery. The more serious crimes, such as murder, were tried before a district court.

There was a case of murder and one subsequent hanging at each of the three county seats. The first public execution by hanging at Salisbury was in 1816 for the murder of a man named Chambers by his father-in-law, Henry Chryst (or Crist). Mrs. Chamber, Chryst's daughter, had complained of her husband's abuse to her father. He confronted Chambers and attacked him with a butcher knife. Chambers ran away, and Chryst grabbed the gun that hung over the door. He chased after his son-in-law, shot him and killed him. Chryst was arrested and jailed at Salisbury.

Witnesses who testified against him were his wife, his young son, the daughter who was married to Chambers and a neighbor who witnesses the killing. Chryst was convicted and sentenced to be hanged. Crowds of people from the remotest parts of other counties came to see the hanging.

In April 1816, Chryst was brought to the gallows in a wagon, seated on his coffin. The wagon was drawn from under him and he was hanged. His son, who had been compelled to provide testimony against his father, came to take the body away. He carried it on a sled and, traveling alone for ten or twelve miles, buried the body in an unknown grave.

The costs for expenses to guard him and diet him (provide meals) and for the gallows and coffin are recorded in the October 12, 1816 minutes of the commissioners' meeting. The cost for the execution added up to about $150.

The second hanging occurred in 1822 at Centerville. Hampshire Pitt killed William Mail, both black men. A fight occurred concerning Pitt's common-law wife when he suspected Mail of having improper relations with her. In the confrontation, Pitt took out a knife and stabbed Mail in the heart. Pitt was promptly arrested and placed in the old log jail in Centerville. He was tried and found guilty. Two of the associate judges, McLane and Davenport, granted him a new trial over the objections of Judge Eggleston. Again he was found guilty and sentenced to hang.

According to writers of the first volume of *History of Wayne County, Indiana*, the execution day was very unpleasant: "Thousands of men, women and children came to witness the hanging. Again the man was brought to hang in a cart. There was not a trap door, only the cart was drawn from under him and he was left to die a slow death."

Pitt was fearful of doctors buying his body for dissection. He engaged a black man he thought was a friend to see that his body was kept from physicians. Pitt gave his horse for payment, but instead of carrying out his instructions, the man sold the body for ten dollars. When Pitt found out about it, he sent for another friend, Christopher Roddy, and begged him to take charge of his body and keep it from being taken by the physicians. Roddy agreed.

After the body was cut down, Roddy brought up a cart carrying a coffin, and a physician came with a wagon without a coffin. An argument and scuffle followed. The physician and Roddy struggled and tugged at the body. Roddy's hold was stronger, and he wrestled it away from the physician. He took the body and buried it on his land in Salisbury.

Roddy decided that the burial site was too obvious. Fearing that the grave would be robbed, he took the body up at night and moved it to a location about seven miles away. The hidden site was located in a dense wood. Roddy buried the body and cut down several trees to cover the spot. The physicians never found it.

Both Salisbury and Centerville had experienced an unfortunate event of capital punishment. It would be more than forty-four years before the last and most dramatic public execution would take place in Richmond.

THE FIRST BATTLE IS OVER

In October 13, 1817, the question of the county seat location was brought before the circuit court, which convened at Salisbury. The question was put before the court, with Honorable John Test presiding plus two associates,

Jesse Davenport and William McLean. Judge Test was absent when they deliberated. The two judges were divided as to where the court should be held. The controversy lingered.

The next term of the circuit court was in March 1818. It met in Centerville and was not moved back. The question was again brought before the court by the eminent attorney Daniel J. Caswell, Esq. The judges still could not agree and issued this statement:

> *A motion having been yesterday made to the Court to determine whether they would hold their present session at Salisbury or Centreville, as doubts have arisen as to the Seat of Justice in this County...The Court decree and determine that the Seat of Justice was permanently established in Salisbury and having been established in Salisbury and the Act of December 21, 1816, not having a sufficient repealing clause, has not removed it, but that the Act of January 28, 1818, authorizes the Court to hold their pro tempore session in the town of Centerville until the legislature should otherwise direct.*

This left the question of the county seat just as confused as ever. It affirmed that the permanent location of the county seat was in Salisbury but that the court was to be temporarily held in Centerville. The *Indiana Gazetteer* of 1850 reported that the question of whether the seat of justice of Wayne County should be at Salisbury or Centerville was contested in the Indiana legislature from 1817 to 1822.

A number of other important measures were being considered by the legislature at that time, and the *Gazetteer* went on to note that "while a subject was being considered, the advocates of it would go around and scare up the Wayne County delegation to try to get them to vote in favor of it." The Wayne County delegates were induced for "a consideration," which was probably to vote for the proposed legislation. However, as often as not, a Wayne County delegate would contribute to "undo the mischief he had helped forward" by either absence on the final vote or by changing his vote at the last minute.

The last struggle between Centerville and Salisbury occurred in 1820. The advocates for Centerville continued to raise the question, and the Salisbury faction continued to oppose the move. Finally, five outside commissioners were appointed by the legislature to meet at the courthouse in Centerville on the first Monday in April 1820. They were to consider all of the laws, acts, testimony and other information that would help make a final decision. However, no arguments from lawyers on either side were to be heard or admitted.

Four of the five commissioners showed up at Centerville. "Thus guarded from the mystification of lawyers on the one hand, and bribery on the other," according to the *Centerville Wayne County Record*, the commissioners were directed to settle the problem and submit their findings in writing to the legislature. After a week of listening to all of the testimony and looking

David Hoover (inset) and the desk he used at the Salisbury courthouse. *Photo by Edward Lafever.*

at all the laws and acts, the commissioners were equally divided as to where the legal county seat should be located. They could find no agreement, and so the matter was left the same as when they began their investigation.

Salisbury was finally vanquished from the county seat battle in Wayne County when all county business was moved to Centerville. The remaining holdout was David Hoover, Wayne County clerk, who refused to move his office from Richmond to Centerville. David Hoover was reelected several times from 1817 to 1831 but steadfastly refused to move. He finally removed himself as clerk of the court due to the fact that he was required "by the people" to operate the office in Centerville.

Salisbury Is Lost to History

As soon as it appeared that the county seat would no longer remain in Salisbury, many of the professional men, lawyers and doctors moved either to Centerville or Richmond. Businesses relocated and people moved their homes. The great hope for Salisbury to become a rich and important town was quickly extinguished. Sometime during the late 1830s, the town totally disappeared because of losing the county seat.

John Scott had a printing business and newspaper in Centerville in the 1820s. He published the first *Indiana Gazetteer* in 1826. One of the earliest maps of Indiana was printed in the book. In Wayne County, the towns of Richmond, Washington (Greens Fork), Economy and Centreville (old spelling) are shown. He shows the county's lack of interest in Salisbury by leaving it off the map, just a few years after the county seat was moved.

It would be remiss not to mention the birth of one of Indiana's most honored men, Oliver P. Morton. Morton was born in Salisbury in 1823. His parents died while he was quite young. He moved to Centerville, where he was apprenticed to a half-brother in the hatter trade. Morton's education began in the Wayne County Seminary at Centerville. When he had finished his studies at the seminary, he enrolled at Miami University in Oxford, Ohio. He did not complete his course of study but instead returned to Centerville to study law.

Morton married in 1845 and was admitted to the bar in 1846. He rose quickly in his profession and played an important role in Indiana and Wayne County's history.

Salisbury Memorial Stone, erected by the Daughters of the American Revolution, 1924. *Photo by Edward Lafever.*

The planners of Centerville prepared for it to become the most important town in the county. The streets were made one hundred feet wide, and as the town grew, so did the need for a narrower street to make more lots. When the streets were narrowed, several arches were built on Main Street to allow the public to reach the houses and businesses behind the front row.

The Centerville brick courthouse and the jail were the only county buildings in use by about 1822–23. The last reference to the Salisbury brick courthouse comes from May 1827. John Sutherland and John Kirby were each paid twenty dollars for "superintending the building of the Court House in Salisbury."

The old records sometimes express statements in a way that may be misunderstood. For instance, the records often state that a contract is "sold" to the builder rather than saying that the bid was accepted. Also, paupers or people who could not support themselves were "farmed out" to the lowest bidder. Thus it may be that the two men "superintending the building" refers to them overseeing the dismantling of it.

The Salisbury brick courthouse was no longer of any value to the county. On the day in 1827 when it was offered for sale, John C. Kibbey, Esq., appeared on behalf of Samuel Woods, the man who had given the land for the courthouse. Kibbey protested against the sale but was ignored, and the building sold for fifty dollars to Thomas Beard. The land, however, did revert back to Woods. The building was torn down, and the bricks used to build other structures in Richmond.

In 1823, a mystifying event was recorded, according to the commissioners' records: "Ordered that John Jones, Esq. draw on the County Treasurer for the sum of Two Hundred Dollars for the purpose of defending the rights of the county against the claim of Levi Purviance." The suit went on for a couple of years, but there is no explanation of its outcome. Several hundred dollars were paid to more than one lawyer for handling the case, and this was a great expense for the county.

CHAPTER 6

COUNTY SEAT BUSINESS IN CENTERVILLE

In September 1824, an elected board of justices met at the Centerville courthouse to conduct county business. Later written history refers to these men as justices of the peace. Apparently, the state legislature enacted a ruling that the justices of the peace should conduct county business instead of three commissioners. The first count was fourteen judges at the meeting of the board. During the time they served, from 1824 to September 1829, the attendance varied from as few as seven to as many as twenty. It would be understandable if little was accomplished in the county during this unsteady attendance. However, the number attending did not seem to stop county business from getting done.

The brick courthouse in Centerville was reported as being shoddily built. Although it was deemed to have been just like the Salisbury brick, there were a large number of repairs made to it as early as early as 1823, when it had barely been completed. Fairly large amounts were spent: $12.00 for nails, $8.00 for shingles and $17.23 for repairs. About $200.00 was spent in May 1824, plus $50.00 for paint, $13.17 for repairs and $186.04 for painting the courthouse. Several other amounts were paid to repair and replace broken windows and fix the shutters and the cupola.

On January 28, 1827, the board of justices enacted an order to build the Wayne County Seminary as instructed by the state legislature. Indiana was a leader in planning for education of children in its earliest laws. A system of taxation was set up to fund the county school.

The seminary project started on March 24, 1828. The brick building was located in Centerville on Lots 100 and 101. It was two stories high, with side walls sixteen inches thick and twenty-one and a half feet high. Four fireplaces heated the building, one at each end on both floors. The first floor was divided into three sections, with nine-inch-thick brick walls. The seminary was the principal school in the county, with several small schools located in some of the townships. It was used until 1853, when it was purchased by the Methodists and maintained as the Whitewater College.

A more substantial jail had been constructed in Centerville to replace the first one, and a building was built for the clerk's and recorder's offices. A wooden fence enclosed the jail and courthouse. A "necessary," the outdoor public restroom of the time, was constructed on the public square near the courthouse. It was "6 ft. x 8 ft with a partition through the same, pit to be dug 4 ft. deep with a door to each apartment. Good materials and finished in a workman like manner." Jacob Drisher was paid $13.50 to build the necessary. It was not long before this structure needed repairs. A necessary was also built for the jail.

The public square in Centerville was quite large, and in order not to waste the valuable property and help support the county, parts of it were leased for business purposes. In 1829, the citizens of Centerville were given permission

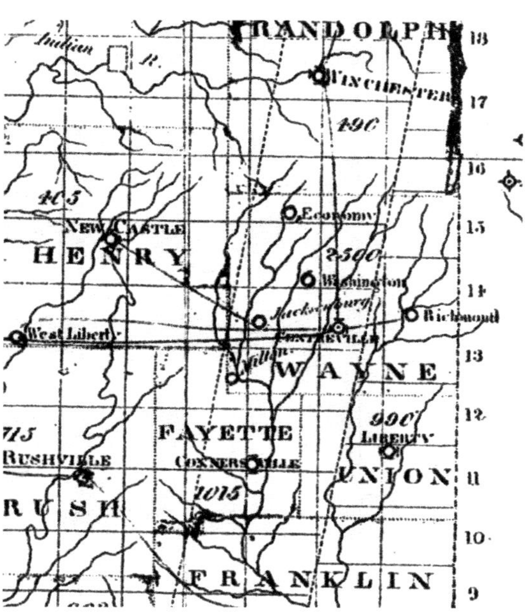

A map of Wayne County, 1826, from the *First Indiana Gazetteer*. Salisbury was left out.

to use a portion of the public square to build a market house. The public square would be recognized today as stretching from the corner of Main and Morton Streets, north to Plum Street and east to First Street, which is about two blocks total.

At the January 1829 session of the state legislature, an act was passed to change the mode of doing county business in the counties of Wayne, Jefferson, Ripley and Fountain:

> *Be it enacted by the General Assembly of the state of Indiana, That there shall be, and hereby is organized in the counties of Wayne, Jefferson, Ripley and Fountain, a board of commissioners for transacting county business, to consist of three qualified electors of said counties, one of whom shall be elected annually to continue in office three years, and until his successor shall be chosen and qualified.*
>
> *...The commissioners so elected shall be paid two dollars per day each, for their services out of their respective county treasuries.*

On September 7, 1829, the board of commissioners was reinstated. Jonathan Platts, Daniel Reid and Jesse Willits provided their certifications of election as commissioners and were seated.

In November 1829, the commissioners allowed $600 of county money to be loaned for one year. Up to $100 per person was allowed. In 1830, Samuel Hanna leased two lots, forty-five feet wide, at the east end of the public square. He was given a fifty-year lease, paying $4 per lot each year, to be reevaluated every ten years. That same year, he was issued a license to keep a tavern on that property. In 1832, James Wood leased a lot on the public square for thirty years at $15 per year.

In May 1831, Wayne County was divided into three commissioners' districts. Much of the business transacted was issuing of business licenses, allowing for the construction of new roads or horse carts and continuing repairs to the courthouse. Taxes were collected either in money or as work on road building and repair.

In September, the state legislature passed an act for the building of state roads. A road was ordered to be built between Washington (Greens Fork) and New Castle, to be no more than forty feet wide. This was eventually connected to Richmond and became State Road 38.

The Indiana legislature enacted many bills that rapidly improved the court system. The first report in the commissioners' books of a person being fined for disturbing the peace and appearing before the Wayne County Circuit Court was dated January 1832. These first circuit court record books are dated 1829–33. District circuit courts had come to the county at regular intervals to hear legal issues.

From its earliest days, Wayne County had appointed overseers for the poor. The county records often mentioned moneys paid to individuals for the care of an orphan or attending a terminally ill person and providing for their burial. Many payments were made for the care of paupers, as recorded in the commissioners' books. These were probably destitute adults who had no means of support. Sometimes paupers were farmed out or given over to an individual for a year, with the county bargaining for the lowest payment he would take. For instance, Daniel Berry was sold (or given for work for a year) for thirty-two dollars, and Thomas Anderson was sold for twenty-four dollars. These may have been underage orphans.

The year 1832 was an important one for the county. The commissioners order a county asylum or poorhouse to be built. In 1912, the location was described as the Wayne County Poor Asylum, situated on a 130-acre farm just north of the National Road and about two miles west of the town of Centerville. The description of this building was a brick and stone building, fifty feet square and twenty feet high.

The location of the first site for the farm is not recorded in the commissioners' books. However, further research revealed the first place to be in Jefferson Township. That farm was sold when the one in Center Township was built. Several expenses were listed for the asylum, such as furnishings, heating fuel and food supplies, beginning in 1832.

CHAPTER 7

RICHMOND OUTGROWS CENTERVILLE

The battle for the courthouse and county seat had subsided. The lawyers and doctors moved out of Salisbury to Centerville and Richmond. Businesses also moved, and the small village faded away.

Centerville was prospering, but a rival was growing nearby. Richmond's second newspaper, the *Public Leger*, boasted on March 6, 1824 that

> *the town now contains, by the census taken this week, 453 inhabitants, principally mechanics…8 Dry goods Stores, 3 large and respectable Taverns, a Post Office, a Printing Office…7 blacksmiths, 4 hatters, 4 cabinet makers, 6 shoe-makers, 3 tailors, 3 coopers, 3 potters, 1 gunsmith…a steam distillery, besides a large number of carpenters, brick and stone masons, plasterers, etc.…of professional men there are but two—physicians; of lawyers we have not one, although every other town in the state abounds with them.*

Richmond's industry of 1824 also included twenty mills within a two-mile radius of the town. The fast-flowing waterways around Richmond provided a source of power for all types of mills.

Richmond continued to outgrow any town in Wayne County. It was incorporated in 1818, which allowed for the election of town officials and the collecting of taxes. In 1827, Isaac Reed traveled through Indiana and recorded his impressions. He visited many places, including Wayne County. He stated that "Richmond is a small but neat town, inhabited principally by Friend Quakers."

Another important contribution to Richmond's growth was that its name had become known to Quakers in all parts of the country. Yearly gatherings of the Friends met in Richmond, and people came from distant states to attend. In his *Life and Travels*, Addison Coffin, a North Carolina Quaker, tells of coming to Richmond in 1843: "Richmond, Indiana, I had been taught from my childhood was the great center of Carolina emigration, and the Jerusalem of Quakerism for all the northwest, and at last I have lived to see it in all its quiet sunset beauty."

AGRICULTURE ADDS WEALTH

Farms in Wayne County were an important part of the county's wealth. They produced large crops of corn and raised hogs, cattle and poultry, as well as other agricultural crops. The only way to get merchandise to market was either by waterways or by primitive trails and roads. Wayne County had no waterways that could be used to ship produce. Hogs and turkeys were taken to market by driving the herds and hoping that very few animals would be taken by predators or get loose. Several men and boys went along on the drives to protect the herds and watch for human thieves along the way. With no protection from law authorities, travelers had to take care of themselves when moving through the countryside and into Ohio with valuable goods.

Prices for farm products were unsteady, and overproduction became a problem. In the early 1820s, prices dropped dramatically. This caused a severe depression in Wayne County, due mostly to the lack of good shipping. According to a historical account written about those times by Dr. John Plummer in 1857, "The croakers among us, as they were technically called… declared Richmond has reached its zenith—there is nothing to keep it up—you will see it decline…when you have raised your corn and your hogs and ground your grain, how are you to get out from here to a market?"

The principal cities for market were Cincinnati or Hamilton, Ohio. Before canals and railroads, most of the surplus produce of Wayne County and surrounding counties had to be hauled by wagons and teams. Storekeepers used the barter system to take produce, including flour, eggs, bacon, lard and dried fruit, in exchange for other goods. The merchants would send the extra to market. Farmers had wagons and teams and could use the hauling fees to pay off their credit with the storekeepers.

Branson Harris wrote in 1914 of his recollections of a hauling trip to Cincinnati about 1835:

> *My father had a large four-horse wagon and two good wheel horses and a near neighbor had two very good horses that worked well in the lead…The neighbor, Mr. Veal, delighted in being on the road with a team…Father made arrangements for me to go along with him to take care of the team on the road. For two or three years after father and Mr. Veal rigged up a team I went to and from Cincinnati with Mr. Veal with the team after harvest till cold weather. We took our provisions with us, and most of the time took horse feed, too.*
>
> *We camped at night and slept in our wagon…In those days there were more or less deep mud holes. We frequently would mire down, and then we would have to double team* [with other drivers] *and get some poles or rails and pry up and pull out, and sometimes help pull each other up steep or long muddy hills.*
>
> *The last trip I made with Mr. Veal…was in the dead of winter. Before we got to Cincinnati weather became warm and rainy…it took all day to unload and gather up our load to take back with us…We then had to go about one mile to where we could stay all night…I got muddy to my knees wading through the slush and mud by the time we got to the wagon yard where we could stay all night.*
>
> *Next morning it was still warm and rainy and foggy…The roads were a perfect "loblolly." I don't know any better word to describe it…It turned cold in the afternoon and froze up solid. That night we could not untie the horses' tails. Next morning everything was frozen up pretty solid. Our wagons stood about felloe deep* [up to the rims] *in mud in the evening and were frozen fast in the morning. We had to take a mattock* [type of heavy pick] *and old axes and dig and chop the wagon wheels loose before we could pull out of the wagon yard. Another such day's teaming as we had during that entire day I never experienced before or since.*
>
> *The road we went that day had a good many low places where the water stood and had frozen over…The weather remained severely cold until we got home. This trip to Cincinnati satisfied my ambition for teaming. It took us ten days to make the trip.*

Branson Harris's experience clearly shows how difficult it was to take produce to market. The need for good roads was evident. The State of Indiana was making plans for internal improvements, which were intended to bring better times.

A National Road

As early as 1784, George Washington had urged for the necessity of a public highway over the mountains to the west. In the early days of the new nation, people traveled on foot, horseback, stagecoach or wagon, and most heavy goods were shipped by water. At the urging of President Jefferson, Congress passed legislation in 1803 that contracted to build a road over the Allegheny Mountains to connect the eastern states with the western territories. A commission was appointed to select the route for the road. The report was completed in 1805, and the work began in 1811.

Building this first road supported by federal funds stirred up a lot of controversy. During the years of President James Madison's administration (1809–17), the work was greatly delayed. At times, the road construction was stopped or slowed because of opposition from people in the eastern states. They objected to contributing to the lure of migration from the Atlantic states because it took money and business away.

Physical force was used against the road construction by demolishing or greatly damaging what had already been built. Walls were torn down and banks were dug away, and help was needed just to protect the road workers.

Finally, in 1822, Congress passed a bill to protect and repair the Cumberland Road—the original name for the National Road. The bill called for tollgates and a fixed schedule of tolls. Anyone who refused to pay the tolls was liable for severe punishment. President James Monroe vetoed the bill, but Congress pressed ahead and appropriated $30,000 for repairing the road.

In 1829, the *Richmond Public Leger* announced that Jonathan Knight, official surveyor for the road, had "completed the location to this place (Richmond). He is now engaged between this and Centerville, which is also made a point." The coming of the road brought excitement to merchants and farmers who could foresee increased trade and migration to the area.

In 1829, contracts for clearing the trees and preparing a roadbed were let out to local contractors. Contracts were given to the lowest bidders, but not more than ten miles were given to any one contractor. No advances of money were to be made, and no bonds for performance were required. As soon as the contracts were given, the work started.

In 1832, Congress appropriated $100,000 to complete work on the Cumberland Road through Indiana, including bridges over the east and west forks of the Whitewater River. The bridge work started in 1833. A large double covered bridge was built over the west fork of the Whitewater, west of Richmond, and was completed in 1834–35. It was an object of admiration for those who traveled the road, as well as the residents of Richmond.

The superstructure of the bridge was built of wood, weatherboarded, planed, covered and painted with three coats of white lead paint. There was an overhang of eight feet on each end. Several different types of contractors were needed. Stonemasons and brick masons, carpenters, loggers and ditch diggers found employment. It was hard, backbreaking work. Considerable skill and knowledge went into this massive road construction and the building of the strong bridges.

Before the Whitewater bridge was built, horses and wagons had to cross the stream south of the location of the Starr Piano Factory (now a historic site in Richmond). Sarah Wrigley, the first librarian of Morrison-Reeves Library, described the harrowing trip down and up the steep banks and through the water of the old ford:

> *The highway from the west descended to the valley by way of a road cut in the hillside and terminated just at the ford below where the Starr Piano factory is situated. This was one of the most reliable and safe fords on the Whitewater.*
>
> *At this point the river flowed over a bed of limestone…The road ascended the hill at a steep incline…east to Fourth street, north on Fourth, and east to the state line.*

In order to continue going west from Richmond, the only way to cross the river was at the ford. It was especially challenging during times of rain and mud. The new covered bridge was greeted with great joy concerning the ease of being able to pass over the river. It was a two-way bridge, allowing traffic to flow in both directions.

CANALS

Both Centerville and Richmond benefited when plans for internal improvements were made public. From 1826, economic conditions had begun to improve in Indiana. The price of land and products went up, and there was an increase in population. In 1832, Indiana's plans for internal improvements were underway. Work was started on the Wabash and Erie Canal. By the middle of the summer of 1835, thirty-two miles of it were complete, with boats making regular runs.

In 1836, other public works were undertaken. The Whitewater Canal was surveyed from Lawrenceburg at the Ohio River north to Brookville. Twenty-three miles of the Central Canal was built through Indianapolis, and twenty miles of a southern division of the Central Canal extending from Evansville was under contract. The crosscut canal from Terre Haute was under contract, and a report was issued for the proposed route of the Michigan and Erie Canal. Contracts were given for the Madison and Lafayette Railroad. Other contracts were let out for surveying, grading and bridging several roads. Indiana had taken on a huge amount of public works at great expense.

Times were good for the people of Wayne County during the 1830s. The opening of the Cumberland Road made Richmond, at the Indiana and Ohio border, the gateway for migrants moving west. As Richmond grew in size and numbers, it quickly surpassed Centerville as the leading town in Wayne County.

In 1834, Richmond petitioned for a more efficient government than was available to town trustees. At a special session of the Indiana legislature in 1834, a borough charter was granted. On March 13, 1834, the first town officers were elected under this charter. This charter governed the town until 1840, when it became a city. Becoming a city allowed for electing a mayor and establishing a city council. In 1843, Richmond's population was estimated at 2,500 and Centerville's population, about 1,000.

Although Centerville did not grow as fast as Richmond, it did have many other advantages. It boasted the courthouse, county offices and the county jail. The county seminary was thriving and was considered an outstanding educational institution. Three doctors and nine lawyers practiced there in 1843. Taverns and inns were built along the National Road. The historic Mansion House was opened in 1840, a huge, four-story tavern and inn. Many shops, blacksmiths, carpenters and other professions flourished in the town.

The intellectual climate was not neglected, either. The Centerville Musical Institute existed about 1840 and owned musical instruments worth $500. The Whitewater Seminary had a fine reputation. Literary societies were organized, such as a historical society, formed by local woman. George Julian was the founder of the group called the Dark Lyceum. This club was formed as a debating society, which gave opportunity to the shy George Julian to practice public speaking. Another of citizens' ambitions was to establish a library. Although the Lyceum started with only two members, it soon grew to include many of the young men in and around Centerville.

John Parsons of Petersburg, Virginia, stopped in Centerville in 1839. There he met John Finley (author of the poem "The Hoosier Nest") and George Julian, a young lawyer and founder of the Lyceum. Parsons and the others attended the Lyceum at the weekly six o'clock evening meeting at the courthouse. The public was invited, and many people attended.

The Lyceum program was a debate among the men of the society, usually about slavery and the rights of suffrage in the state. Both sides of the issue were debated. Congressman George Julian and Governor Oliver Morton gave credit to their participation in the Lyceum for helping them learn to speak well before the public.

John Parsons described the Lyceum meeting at the courthouse, which was the second one built in Centerville.

> *The scene was an interesting one. The western window and the early hour of meeting made candle-light unnecessary in the early part of the evening, and the rays of the setting sun shone in upon the intent faces of the gathering, some in staid Quaker garments, others in worldly clothing of fine broadcloth with high stocks and ruffled shirt fronts, and I had to admit to myself that nothing more enhances female beauty than the dove-colored garments and snowy kerchief prescribed the religion of the Friend.*

The courthouses in Centerville were used for public meetings, as well as the sessions of the courts and commissioners. Church groups were allowed to meet in the building. Meetings of social societies also used the large rooms.

When the first courthouse of brick was constructed in Centerville, it appeared to be a most substantial building. However, the commissioners' records show a continuous need and expense for repairs at the courthouse.

Enoch Railsback, writing for the *Indiana Radical* in 1869, related his witness to the demise of the first Centerville courthouse. The building was a cheaply constructed building and later became unsafe. Railsback was present at an exciting election for the local congressman. The count was close, and the house was filled with men and boys waiting for the election results. The overcrowded and unsteady floor gave way and sunk about twelve inches, giving quite a fright to those attending. According to Railsback, "Each person within made it his special business to hunt an opening in which he might escape injuries from the fallen building. The excitement was great but nobody was seriously hurt although a few were knocked down and thoroughly trampled over."

This courthouse was not used after this event, which took place in the fall of 1832. All county business was moved to the local Methodist church until the fourth courthouse could be constructed.

CHAPTER 8

SECOND COURTHOUSE IN CENTERVILLE

In early 1833, the board of commissioners contracted with William Commons to build a new courthouse in Centerville. He was to receive $5,000 and the old building. Philip Savill and Lot Bloomfield would oversee the building of the courthouse. This was the second courthouse in Centerville and the fourth in the county.

The board received the finished courthouse in May 1835. William Commons received his pay in increments of $1,000.00 over four years. In 1837, Commons was paid $17.97 for sand hauled to pave the courthouse yard.

When the new courthouse was completed in Centerville, both Centerville and Richmond were doing well. People were employed and rapidly bought up lots for homes and business. Mills and factories were on the rise, and flourishing farms added to the wealth in the county. Centerville had been important enough to have a portion of the National Road paved through the center of town. The new covered bridge over the Whitewater River improved the road traffic.

Since Richmond's population was more than double Centerville's, ideas of once more moving the county seat were being considered. In 1843, the *Centerville Wayne County Record* praised Richmond as having "handsome streets, beautiful private residences, splendid hotels and public buildings." The *Record* continued by pointing out other attributes of its neighbor: "Richmond exhibits more taste, beauty and adornment, than any other town in the County, and probably, in this respect, had but few rivals in the State."

The second courthouse in Centerville. *Courtesy of Jack Phelps.*

Wayne County was excited about the internal improvement program initiated by the state government. As part of the program, canals headed the list. The Whitewater Canal, to be built in the eastern center of the state, was believed to be a solution to the landlocked areas needing better ways to export goods. Construction of the White Water Canal began at Brookville in 1836.

The future for towns located along the canal route looked promising. The work provided employment for a large number of men. There were several canals in other parts of the country being built at the same time, and good workers were scarce. A man could make a good wage working for canal companies. During the first season of building the Whitewater Canal, teams of men and horses were estimated to equal the work of 975 men. Among the canal workmen were 325 of European decent, many of them Irish.

Citizens of Richmond also desired to benefit from a canal that would connect to the Whitewater Canal at Brookville. The Richmond and Brookville Canal Company was organized in 1838. About $45,000 was spent on the project when the flood of January 1847 washed out most of the completed construction. The backers saw their money disappear, and the project was abandoned.

A Dream Is Washed Away

By 1839, the Whitewater Canal was about half finished from Brookville to Cambridge City. The section south of Brookville was open and in operation. But the grand plans for Indiana's internal improvements had to be abandoned as the debt increased far beyond what the state could pay. In November 1839, the Indiana legislature ordered "that with the exception of the Wabash canal, from Lafayette to the State line, and the dams on other works yet to be preserved, the work at Lawrenceburg and bridges at Harrison, the public works be immediately suspended."

It was obvious that the state would have to give up. The legislature realized that it could not pay the interest money on a debt estimated to be more than $13 million. It abolished the board of internal improvements, which had been in charge of the public works, and made provision to transfer some of the projects to private companies.

Not only was the state bankrupt and promises of public works went unfulfilled, but also many private companies and individuals were deeply in debt. The people along the canal route had anticipated great fortunes. Sites were selected for large cities. Streets and building lots were laid out. Merchants expanded and ordered goods that they could not pay for. However, hopes remained high when private companies formed to complete the canal construction.

In order to finish the work on the canal, the Whitewater Valley Canal Company was chartered in 1842 with a capital of $400,000. The company owned the entire canal from Cambridge City to the Ohio River. The first boat reached Cambridge City in October 1845.

Originally, Hagerstown, located north of Cambridge City in Wayne County, was to have been the upper end of the Whitewater Canal, to be built along the Nettle Creek. Residents there did not want to be left out of the prosperity that would come with transportation on the canal. There were no state funds available, but local residents believed that it was important to complete the last seven miles of the canal to their town.

The Hagerstown Canal planners did not rush into the canal-building project without giving it serious thought. German Baptists or Dunkards, known as a conservative yet progressive group, made up a substantial part of the population. A study was made of the canal route, and care was taken to make it less vulnerable to floods than the sections south.

In 1846, the Hagerstown Canal company was formed with strong community backing. From start to finish, the Hagerstown Canal was paid for, operated and controlled by the Hagerstown company. It was reported the Dunkards brought their horse teams and worked beside the hired men without any pay for their work.

Not everyone was happy about the canal. Solomon and Benjamin Zehner had built a mill on the Nettle Creek waterway south of Hagerstown. Benjamin ran the farm and handled the money. Solomon ran the mill. The ditch for the canal came very close to the mill.

In 1847, the Hagerstown Canal was placed so that a boat could barely pass between the Zehner mill and the opposite bank. One morning, the Irish canal workers came to take out the dam, which was protecting the mill. As might be expected, the Zehners were not going to allow their mill to be ruined. The two wives came out with tea kettles of hot water and the men with guns. The workers were forced to leave and go into Hagerstown. According to the story, the workers got drunk, came back and removed the dam. The water overflowed and the mill stood in five feet of water.

The matter was taken to court, but nothing was resolved until many years later when Benjamin Zehner received some damages. The mill was abandoned when the canal was completed. Later it was converted into a sawmill. Nothing remains today of the mill site. The mill stood on the grounds that later became the Boy Scout camp of Wapi-Kamigi near the airport in Hagerstown.

While the canal was in operation, it carried both passengers and goods to and from Cincinnati. Farmers brought their produce from as far as Muncie, on poor roads for more than forty miles, to increase profits by shipping it to Cincinnati. Robert and Frank Newcomb owned a large grain mill in Hagerstown. They made a fortune by shipping grain to Russia for use in the Crimean War in 1853–54.

The Whitewater Canal was plagued with problems of heavy rains, causing floods to wash out the banks and dams. At first, things seemed to be going well, and the prospects of wealth pointed to ever-increasing prosperity in the Whitewater Valley.

In 1847, a great flood carried away the aqueduct across Symond's creek near Cambridge City and the one across the west fork of Whitewater at Laurel. The cost was over $100,000 to the company.

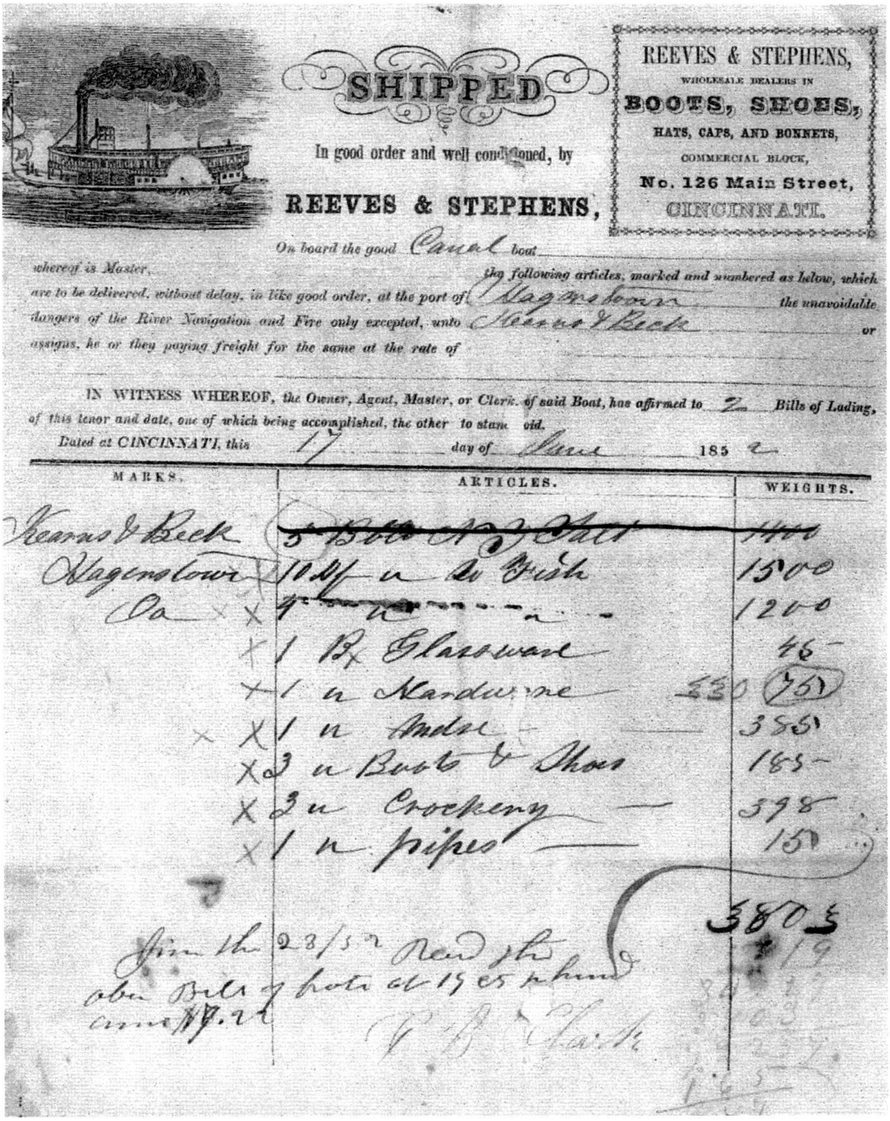

SHIPPED

In good order and well conditioned, by

REEVES & STEPHENS,

REEVES & STEPHENS,
WHOLESALE DEALERS IN
BOOTS, SHOES,
HATS, CAPS, AND BONNETS,
COMMERCIAL BLOCK,
No. 126 Main Street,
CINCINNATI.

On board the good Canal *boat*
whereof is Master, *the following articles, marked and numbered as below, which are to be delivered, without delay, in like good order, at the port of* Hagenstown *the unavoidable dangers of the River Navigation and Fire only excepted, unto* Kearns & Beck *or assigns, he or they paying freight for the same at the rate of*

IN WITNESS WHEREOF, *the Owner, Agent, Master, or Clerk of said Boat, has affirmed to* 2 *Bills of Lading, of this tenor and date, one of which being accomplished, the other to stand void.*

Dated at CINCINNATI, this 17 *day of* June 1852

MARKS.	ARTICLES.	WEIGHTS.
Kearns & Beck	~~5 Bbls N. Y. Salt~~	~~1400~~
Hagenstown	10 Hf [illegible] Fish	1500
Pa	~~4 [illegible]~~	1200
	1 Bx Glassware	45
	1 " Hardware	75
	1 " [illegible]	38
	3 " Boots & Shoes	185
	2 " Crockery	598
	1 " pipes	150
		3803

Jun the 23/52 Recd the above Bill of Goods at 1.9 cts ... amt $7.22

C. B. Clark

A Whitewater Canal shipping document. 1852. *Courtesy of the Wayne County Historical Museum.*

The repairs were barely finished when a second flood in November 1848 caused $80,000 of damage. If it had not been for farmers of the valley raising money for the repairs, the canal would have been abandoned. The final death knell of the canal sounded in 1853 when a third flood tore out the repairs and caused more damage.

The last boat to Hagerstown ran in 1861. In 1863, the Whitewater Railroad purchased the towpath of the canal. The railroad carried freight and passengers throughout the area for several years.

Remnants of the White Water Valley railroad and the Whitewater Canal can be visited today in Connersville and Metamora. Patrons can ride on the train from Connersville to Metamora, where one can take a short ride on a canal packet.

CHAPTER 9

POLITICS, RADICALS AND SLAVERY

During the time the second Centerville courthouse was in use, 1835 to 1873, Wayne County dealt with troubling social issues affecting the whole country. The issue of slavery had been a concern since before Wayne County was established. The antislavery forces seemed to be in control in Indiana, and the problem festered in debates across the country. Northern states insisted that slavery should be abolished. Citizens of Southern states, whose livelihood depended on the cheap labor of slaves, wanted no interference. The debate between the states continued to grow in intensity and would culminate, when compounded by other reasons, in the American Civil War.

The desire to rid the United States of slavery was present as early as the colonial period and the Revolutionary War. Although the laws of the Northwest Territory did not allow it, immigrants from the southern states brought slaves into Indiana. The same laws were applied to the Indiana Territory but were still ignored, especially in the southern counties of the territory.

Indiana's first constitution in 1816 did not allow slavery or indentured servants. The abolitionists had firm control in the state legislature, but the federal census of 1820 shows 190 slaves listed in Indiana. As late as 1840, three slaves were listed in the census. A variety of acts were passed in Congress to allow slaveholders to capture them in the free states. These laws forced abolitionists to come together in several ways to help runaway slaves escape.

Wayne County's most well-known antislavery advocate was Levi Coffin—merchant, abolitionist and temperance leader. Coffin came to Newport (now Fountain City) in Wayne County in 1826. He had been involved with helping slaves in his home state of North Carolina. He and his family were members of the Society of Friends.

Many Friends, or Quakers, had already settled in and around Richmond. The appeal in large part was to come to a state free of slavery and in which Quakers were not harassed and mistreated for their actions against slavery. Wayne County commissioners' records show that Levi Coffin paid ten dollars for a license to vend merchandise in Newport in July 1830.

Coffin opened a store shortly after settling in Newport. He sold a variety of goods—many of them produced by him. He began manufacturing linseed oil in 1836 and paints of various colors. The paint was popular, and many customers bought the paint to decorate their wagons. The quiet gray-and-black Quakers thoroughly disapproved of the brightly colored wagons. According to Henry C. Fox's 1912 history, "The Friends became very much concerned and appointed a committee to labor with him [Coffin] and persuade him to leave off such sinful work."

Helping runaway slaves was carried out in an unorganized way before the 1830s. People in Wayne County felt strongly about getting rid of slavery, but they and others across the country could not agree on the best way to accomplish it. Some Quakers believed in immediate and unconditional emancipation. Others believed that gradual emancipation or some form of colonization would be a better way. But there was agreement that there should be none bound in slavery.

Several antislavery societies were formed across the country and in Indiana. In 1838, the Indiana Anti-Slavery Society was formed at Milton in Wayne County. The local press was not sympathetic to the movement, especially the idea that slave labor goods should be boycotted.

Abolitionists used every means at hand to further their ideas. They formed antislavery societies, sent out speakers and formed their own press. In Newport, two newspapers were issued. The *Protectionist* in 1841 was a weekly paper. In 1843, the *Free Labor Advocate* began its publication. The *Advocate* was published for many years, until its political views were no longer of public interest and the publisher died.

The stronger the antislavery cause became, the more its foes tried to destroy it. According to the *Reminiscences* of Levi Coffin, "It tried a man's soul to be an abolitionist in those days, when brickbats, stones and rotten eggs were some of the arguments we had to meet."

Coffin and his wife, Catharine, opened their home to runaway slaves in Newport from the 1830s to 1847. Goods for his store were shipped by wagon, and he was able to work out ways to carry runaway slaves into and out of Newport. There was a network of supporters on three routes to the Coffin House, from Jeffersonville, Madison and Cincinnati. Free blacks and sympathetic white people opened their homes, giving aid and comfort to the destitute slaves. Because of the secrecy and effectiveness of this work, it was given the name "Underground Railroad."

Helping runaway slaves was costly in lost business and threats of violence. But many Quakers and other religious groups joined the antislavery societies. Methodists and members of the Wesleyan Church formed antislavery societies. They had to take a stand against the leaders of their denominations, many of whom were proslavery. Daniel Worth, a prominent Wesleyan minister in Wayne County, was active in the Indiana Anti-Slavery Society and was at one time its president. Several of the Indiana Anti-Slavery conventions were held at Newport.

Not all Quakers and residents of Newport were abolitionists. The movement of slaves through the safe houses had to be kept secret. Congress passed a law, the Fugitive Slave Act of 1850, that allowed slave hunters to capture runaways in free states. The only people who knew the activities of the safe houses were the ones who gave help to the escaping slaves. The Underground Railroad brought more than two thousand slaves through the home of Levi Coffin during the more than twenty years he lived in Newport.

In 1842, a "Meeting for the Suffering" at the Indiana Yearly Meeting of the Society of Friends was held in Richmond. Conflicts between the antislavery faction and the others of the Society came to a head. Members attending the meeting—Charles Osborn, Jacob Graves, William Lock, Benjamin Stanton and other abolitionists—were prohibited from taking part in the meeting. Humiliated and embarrassed, the antislavery faction met together in the Yearly Meetinghouse near the end of the session. They were ordered to disband or get out of the house. They chose to leave and held a meeting the next day at Newport.

The antislavery Quakers took no further action until February 1843 of the next year. At that time, they separated from the others and formed their own Indiana Yearly Meeting of antislavery Friends.

Henry Fox in the 1912 *Memoirs of Wayne County* describes the attitude of the members of the Yearly Meeting who forced out the antislavery faction:

> *As has been stated before, most Friends believed in freeing the slaves, but could not agree to the method used by the anti-slavery element, since they did not believe in entering into any kind of excitement, but in a quiet, deliberate sort of way. The joining of any kind of a society, such as temperance, anti-slavery or peace, was a step towards excitement.*

During the years of Newport's antislavery activities, another important social issue was being debated. According to the *Centerville Wayne County Record*, in the early 1830s there was an increasing demand for liquor, leading to "drinking, swearing gangs of rowdies about the places of dissipation….quarreling or fighting among themselves." Quakers generally opposed liquor and drunkenness, although some drank beer. Levi Coffin, Henry H. Way and Daniel Pucket agreed to rouse public sentiment against drinking by organizing a temperance society in Newport. There were no other temperance societies in the western states. Because not all Quakers agreed as to the proper use of liquor, the men sought the support of the Methodists. Three men from each denomination met to plan the organization.

The Newport Temperance Society was formed with twelve men signing the pledge. Public acceptance was slow until women decided to join the cause, "which always means strength and encouragement," according to Fox's *Memoirs of Wayne County*.

Public sentiment changed rapidly, and saloon dealers were soon out of business in Newport. Centerville persuaded the county commissioners to deny licenses to vendors of "Ardent Spirits" in town and not to renew those that had expired. In March 1843, the *Centerville Wayne County Record* reported, "For nearly two month past, we have had no establishment in this town, licensed to vend Ardent Spirits."

Two years before, in 1840, the *Wayne County Whig* newspaper reported that a bill had been put up in the state legislature by Mr. Meredith to prevent the retail sale of "Spiritous Liquors" in Dalton Township. Several temperance societies were organized in Wayne County, and their influence was strong.

In the 1880s, taverns that sold bootleg liquors were called "blind tigers." At the same time, hotels advertised "sample rooms," which sold whiskey and other liquors. The battle raged for many years between the Whiskey Party and the temperance societies, eventually leading to the era of Prohibition in the United States (1920–33).

George Julian: An Indiana Radical

The *Centerville Wayne County Record* reported that Wayne County's population in 1841 was 22,983, the largest in Indiana. The production of hogs and wheat was the largest in the state, and it was fourth in producing corn.

Although Centerville was the county seat, it never reached the size and wealth of Richmond. However, because of its educational institutions and its intellectual climate, several outstanding leaders rose to serve in the state legislature and in Congress. Among them were George Julian and Oliver P. Morton.

George Washington Julian, son of Isaac and Rebecca Julian, was born near Centerville in 1817. He was the fourth child in the family of seven children. George was just six years old when his father died. Rebecca and her young family returned to Wayne County after her husband died, and she had enough money to buy a farm. The family worked hard to make a living. Rebecca Julian encouraged in her children a strong religious faith. They were Hicksite Quakers.

The oldest son, John, died when he was just twenty-three. Two of the younger sons, Jacob and George, had successful careers as lawyers. Jacob practiced in Centerville and Indianapolis, later becoming a judge of the Marion Circuit Court. George practiced law for a time with Jacob. He became a distinguished lawyer, statesman and orator. The youngest brother, Isaac, worked for newspapers and published his own in Centerville.

At sixteen years old, George was a strapping six feet two inches tall. He worked at several jobs before he settled into a career. He spent time as a rod man helping the surveyors on the Whitewater Canal and worked a short time on the National Road. He became a teacher at eighteen. While teaching in Illinois, he began to study law.

In 1840, George Julian was admitted to the bar and began practicing in Newcastle and Greenfield. In 1843, George came back to Centerville to join his brother Jacob's law office as a junior partner.

In 1923, Grace Julian Clarke, George Julian's daughter, wrote a biography of her father. She described his career and what it cost to stand up for his beliefs and fight the wrongs he saw in American society.

George Julian was passionate about antislavery and land reform and was against capital punishment. His political party was Whig, the dominant party in Wayne County. In 1845, he worked hard for the election of Henry Clay, making speeches throughout the county. He gained a reputation as an eloquent and effective speaker. That same year, Julian was elected a member of the state legislature from Wayne County. He attracted attention by working for the abolition of capital punishment and other prominent legislative issues.

The Whig Party did not support George's strong views on slavery. No longer able to agree with the Whigs, George went to the convention of the Free-Soil Party in Buffalo, New York, in the fall of 1848. He came away with a burning desire to advocate the antislavery platform in whatever ways he could. He set about traveling and giving speeches two or three times a day, eager to debate the Whig leaders.

This was a time when bitter words were thrown at people—ridiculing, calling them names and threatening. George and his young wife were shunned by friends in Centerville because it was a stronghold for the Whig Party. While George was traveling for his speeches, his wife was often left alone. She was the target of averted glances and shouted jeers. More than one night she was awakened to hear hoodlums yelling, groaning and hooting beneath her window.

The charge of being an abolitionist was thrown at George wherever he went. At this time, the name was meant as a hateful slur. He was called "wooly-head," "apostle of disunion" and the "orator of free dirt," referring to the Free-Soil Party. It was said that he had "negrophobia." He was so disliked by the Whig Party in Centerville that he was threatened with being "ridden out on a rail" and would not have been surprised at any violence against him.

Mrs. Clarke's biography relates many instances of how deeply George and his family were wounded by people of the Whig Party turning against him. In his own words, written in his journal of September 19, 1848, he notes:

> *This day, because I would be a Barnburner* [Van Buren's faction of the New York Democracy who oppose the extension of slavery into the western Territories] *J.B. Julian requested a dissolution of our partnership, to which of course I promptly agreed. I am now thrown*

entirely on my own resources, political and professional…Everything that party tyranny and exasperation can suggest will be done to prostrate me by men who know that I am honest in my convictions and that I could have no sinister motives. And now even a brother, chiming in with the popular clamor, sees proper to join in the general cry of "mad dog." Well, be it so…A better day will come; and believing this, and seeing it with the eye of faith, I shall not despair but thank God and take courage.

The Free-Soil Party did not carry one state in the election of 1848. The effect of his defection from the Whig Party was hard on George's family and his finances, but both husband and wife were willing to face the hardships for what they believed was right.

Events in the United States and Wayne County continued to be agitated and were coming to a boiling point over slavery. In 1850, the Southern states were worried about losing the balance in Congress of one slave state for every free state admitted to the Union. With the taking of territories from

George Julian, 1817–1899.

Mexico, the issue flared up regarding how to divide them into slave and free. Congress worked out a compromise bringing California in as a free state and the rest allowing slaves.

Along with this compromise, the Fugitive Slave Act was passed. It allowed slave owners to go anywhere to recapture runaways. Both free blacks and slaves were fair game for anyone who claimed to be their owners. Blacks had no rights, and with anyone producing a claim of ownership, they could be shipped south back into slavery. This act enraged people in the Northern states and pushed both sides further apart. The Underground Railroad for escaped slaves became even more active.

Harriet Beecher Stowe published her tales of "Uncle Tom's Cabin" in the *National Era*. The stories were enthusiastically received, and she was urged to put them in a book. Many publishers did not want to be associated with abolitionist books, but she found one who would put them into print. The book came out in 1852, and 5,000 copies were sold the first two days. In the first year, 300,000 copies sold in America alone.

One story Mrs. Stowe wrote was based on a true incident. It was the story of a slave woman who passed through the home of Levi Coffin in Wayne County. The book helped fuel passions leading up to the American Civil War.

George Julian continued his work with the Free-Soil Party, denouncing the Fugitive Slave Law. When the Kansas-Nebraska Act passed in 1854, he again went on a speaking campaign to combat this new heresy. The law allowed new states or territories to decide for themselves whether to allow slavery. He was greatly disappointed when a large convention of various political parties in Indianapolis declined to support antislavery, only favoring a return to the Missouri Compromise of 1820. This law allowed one free state for each slave state admitted to the Union, which pacified the strong, Southern block in Congress.

About the same time as antislavery was coming to the forefront of American politics, George Julian was also working on behalf of temperance and the women's rights movement. He was a lifelong supporter of women's and black suffrage.

The Whig and Free-Soil Parties both lost momentum and membership. Some of their memberships came together to form a new Republican Party in the Northern states. Their first candidate for president was Abraham Lincoln in 1860. Wayne County overwhelmingly supported Lincoln.

The slogan for the Republican campaign was "Free labor, Free soil, Free men." Lincoln and Douglas hotly debated slavery and the freeing of the slaves, with Douglas declaring, "I want citizenship for whites only," according to newspaper accounts.

Abraham Lincoln's reply was, "I believe this Government cannot endure permanently half-slave and half-free." The Southern states had other issues such as states' rights, which were at odds with the Republican Party. When Lincoln was elected in 1860, South Carolina was the first to break away from the Union. Ten more states soon followed, and war was declared between the North and South on April 12, 1861.

CHAPTER 10

THE CIVIL WAR AND A NEW COUNTY BATTLE THREATENS

Oliver Morton, Indiana's Civil War governor, was a son of Wayne County. He was born in Salisbury in 1823. After his mother's death, his father moved to Centerville. At fourteen, Morton entered the Wayne County Seminary. He was able to continue his education at Miami University in Oxford, Ohio.

Morton excelled at sports, and he greatly enjoyed extemporaneous debate. Lack of finances kept Morton from completing his studies at the university. Instead, he began to study law in the office of John S. Newman at Centerville. His legal education progressed so well that, five years after passing the bar, the governor appointed him to the circuit court.

His first ten years of political interest was spent as a Democrat, but as he recognized their attitudes against antislavery, he left the party. Although Whig and Free-Soil Parties did not agree on many things, they worked to form a new political party, the Republican Party. Morton was sent as a delegate to the convention at Pittsburgh. Both George Julian and Morton were delegates to this convention. At this time, their views may have been similar, but they were never close friends and eventually became bitter enemies.

Indiana Republicans nominated Morton for governor of Indiana in 1856. He was defeated by the incumbent, Governor Ashbel P. Willard. While considering it a loss at the time, the next four years saw Republicans growing stronger in the state. In 1860, Morton ran for lieutenant governor, with Henry S. Lane running for governor. The plan was that, if elected, Lane would go into the United States Senate and Morton would become governor.

Oliver P. Morton, Indiana's Civil War governor.

The Republicans won by ten thousand votes. Lane moved to the Senate, and Morton became governor of Indiana on January 16, 1961. Hardly had he taken office when, a few days after the war started, Lincoln called for seventy-five thousand men to join the Union army. Morton telegraphed immediately: "On behalf of the State of Indiana, I tender to you for the defense of the Nation and to uphold the authority of the Government, 10,000 men."

Richmond, Centerville, Cambridge City, Hagerstown and other small towns in Wayne County filled their quotas quickly. The volunteers were sent to Indianapolis. Camp Wayne was established on the Richmond fairgrounds to train soldiers. They stayed there until December 10, 1861, when they were sent to the field.

The history of the Civil War is complex, lasting over four years. Much suffering and sacrifice was felt on both sides of the conflict. Indiana and Wayne County played an important part in the war by sending hundreds of volunteers to the army. Wayne County's rich farm fields helped feed the Union army. Great attention was given to help the military families in Wayne County, who suffered from loss of breadwinners and the erratic receipt of soldiers' pay.

Women, men and children of Wayne County rallied around its soldiers to send aid. In 1864, Wayne County received a prize banner presented by the state officers and the State Sanitary Commission. The county had the greatest number of troops enlisted during the preceding year and the largest amount of sanitary supplies forwarded to the troops.

George Julian, serving in Congress, was a leading advocate for antislavery. Newspapers of the county wrote strongly worded articles on both sides of the issue. The *Jeffersonian*, a Democrat paper, was highly critical of the "Abolitionists" who tried to keep the legislature from doing "real business." The *Richmond Palladium* was Republican, and the two editors criticized each other without mercy. Isaac Julian, George's brother, had purchased the *Indiana True Republican* in Centerville. The paper featured many articles on his brother's antislavery activity and speeches.

County business in Wayne County went on quietly during the war years, taking care of the necessary items while supporting the war effort. After the war, county issues came to the forefront. The thirty-year-old courthouse in Centerville needed an upgrade to care for the records, and there was also a need for a new county jail.

The war ended in April 1865. The *Richmond Palladium* reported the enthusiastic reception of the news that Lee had surrendered the Confederate army to General Grant:

> *All business was suspended—business houses closed, and the day given up to rejoicing and making due preparation for bon-fires. With one accord a simultaneous attack was made on the wooden awnings in front of our business-houses on Main St. and sign-posts, and in less time than it takes for us to pen this paragraph, sufficient lumber was piled up at the different cross-streets intersecting Main, to make the largest fires ever before seen in our Quaker city.*

Bonfires, fireworks and speeches filled the streets, as they did in other Wayne County towns. Another *Palladium* article stated that the total damage from the out-of-control bonfire at Richmond was estimated to be thousands of dollars. Several barrels of tobacco being shipped through Richmond by France were destroyed, along with other business and personal property.

After the celebration was over, the United States had to face war debt and the consequences of death and devastation throughout the land. When President Lincoln was assassinated shortly after the war ended, Andrew Johnson became president. Oliver Morton and George Julian both served in Congress under President Johnson. The same party elected both, but their views were very different about the reconstruction of the nation. They both disagreed with Johnson's policies and worked to have him impeached.

By the late 1860s, Julian had moved away from the Republican Party. He took issue with it on matters of war debt and black suffrage. Julian did not run for Congress in 1872 when Grant was elected. By this time, Julian and his family were calling themselves "Liberal Radicals." Isaac Julian brought another paper in Richmond in 1865. He combined the papers and renamed the newspaper the *Indiana Radical*. In 1872, he renamed it *Julian's Radical*, claiming it to be

> *A Paper for the People. This original Anti-Slavery and most Radical paper of Indiana will be found as firm and thoroughgoing as of yore…THE RADICAL is accordingly, devoted to the LABOR MOVEMENT in all its various phases, to Tariff and Finance Reform, to Woman suffrage, Temperance and ADVANCE IDEAS on all subjects.*

As Wayne County affairs moved forward after the war, the board of commissioners in Centerville gave out contracts to build a new sheriff's residence and jail in 1867. In the *Richmond Item* on September 19, 1867, it stated that "the new Centreville jail and Bailiff's dwelling is going up slowly. It will be not only a safe place but an ornament to the county."

According to some of the Richmond newspapers, this was a ploy to keep the county seat in Centerville.

RICHMOND'S CAMPAIGN BEGINS

Richmond had far outstripped Centerville in size, population and business by the end of the Civil War. The census of 1870 reports Richmond to have had 9,445 residents and Centerville, 1,077. From the time the National Road came through Richmond, the city had grown rapidly in population and industry. By the 1850s, Richmond was one of the strong manufacturing centers in Indiana, primarily producing farm equipment. In 1853, the first railroad came through, and by the end of the Civil War, it was the center of manufacturing and commerce of the county. A network of turnpikes and railroads intersected in Richmond. It was the largest and wealthiest city in Wayne County and, in the view of its residents, should become the county seat.

The *Richmond Palladium* printed a report in December 1869 from the auditor of the state. It showed the amount of taxes collected in the six wealthiest counties in Indiana. The tax figures include the amount for the state revenue, the school tax and sinking fund tax. Marion County was first with $274,981.93. Wayne County was second with $104,130.35. For many years, Wayne County had contributed more taxes than several other counties put together.

During the Civil War, state representatives from Richmond had not been idle in trying to have the county seat moved. A series of acts were passed in the state legislature beginning in 1855. They changed some of the older laws, such as the requirement of the county seat to be near the center of the county. The final act needed to push for change was passed on February 24, 1869. This allowed county residents to petition the board of county commissioners to move the county seat. The petition required the signature of 55 percent of legal voters in the county. It would then be up to the commissioners to make the final decision.

The Centerville sheriff's residence and jail were ordered in 1867 and built at the cost of $80,000. A new $10,000 ornamental iron fence was placed around

The sheriff's residence and jail in Centerville, 1867. *Courtesy of the Centerville Center Township Public Library.*

Centerville library, showing the emblem and holes made by the cannon fire over the front door. *Photo by Edward Lafever.*

the county buildings in the public square. Taxpayers in the county protested the cost and agreed that this was an attempt to keep the county seat in Centerville. The protests raised against the excessive expense gave the Richmond party another tool to help pry the county seat away from Centerville.

THE DEBATE HEATS UP

As the debate became more intense, the newspapers were filled with reasons for or against the removal. In order to pressure the commissioners to move the county seat to Richmond, petitions were circulated throughout the county. They were able to collect 4,937 signatures. This was more than the 55 percent needed. The petition was presented to the commissioners in June 1872.

Centerville was prepared with a remonstrance to counteract the petition. A motion was made by attorney William Peelle for a continuance of the question. It was overruled by the commissioners. A deed for a courthouse square in Richmond was presented. The deed would be taken into consideration and examined as to the legality of its title. If everything was in order, an architect would be hired. The governor of the state would be asked to appoint a group of commissioners to assess the value of the county buildings in Centerville. Richmond would have to pay the county for the public buildings as a requirement for moving the county seat.

A challenge was thrown down, and Centerville took up the fight with a vengeance. Articles in the Centerville paper argued that the town would be greatly damaged by the loss. It would be inconvenient for some areas of the county to have to go to Richmond. Centerville citizens accused the Richmond petitioners of getting people from Ohio, Idaho and other states to sign the petition, making it illegal. They threatened to fill their remonstrance by drawing on Ireland, Germany and the tombstones of the county graveyards.

The remonstrance by the Centerville faction had been recognized and rejected. In September 1872, the deed for the public square in Richmond was accepted by the commissioners. The property for relocating the county seat, as well as the Centerville buildings, was paid for by the people of Richmond. Centerville advocates to prevent the removal immediately filed legal proceedings.

The case entered was *William A. Peele v. the Board of Commissioners of Wayne County*. It was heard before Judge Hayes of the circuit court in February 1873. The remonstrators hired Jonathan W. Gordon of Indianapolis, a famous lawyer of his day, to argue their case. William A. Bickle was the lead attorney for the petitioners who wanted to see the county seat moved to Richmond.

Both lawyers represented their sides with long and spirited arguments. Judge Hayes took the case under advisement for two weeks and at the end sent his decision to the board of commissioners. The judgment was in favor of the petitioners and the commissioners' decision to move the county seat.

The remonstrators from Centerville lost this round. The judgment was entered in March 1873.

The county seat was finally declared fixed and located in Richmond. Another injunction was sought, but Judge George Johnson decided for the petitioners, and the books and courthouse belongings would be moved to Richmond.

Contracts were given out for a new Richmond courthouse and jail in March 1873. Thomas W. Roberts was given the contract to build them for $22,500. The governor's commission completed its duty of setting a value to the county buildings in Centerville. They were appraised at $80,000. Richmond made the first payment of $25,000 to the county in April. By August, the courthouse and jail in Richmond were ready to receive the documents, furnishings and prisoners.

The commissioners met in a special session on August 4. They were technically on vacation. Oliver T. Jones, commissioner from the Centerville area district, had voted against the county seat move. He protested but was overruled by the other two commissioners. He did not attend the special session.

The two commissioners, Andrew Wiggins and William Brooks, gave the final acceptance to the courthouse and jail. They met with the sheriff, auditor and other officials and gave orders to move the court records and prisoners that same day. A train of eighteen express wagons proceeded to Centerville to move everything from the courthouse. When the wagons arrived, it created a furor in the town among the people who had come to look. Fourteen of the wagons and teams entered the gates of the Courthouse Square. Before they realized what was happening, a crowd of people closed the gates behind them and fastened them with chains and locks. They were trapped inside.

The sheriff ordered the crowd to desist in the name of the law. According to the *Richmond Times*:

> *A tornado of discord and evil passions arose, making "confusion worse confounded." All of the bells were set to twanging and tinkling, guns and anvils fired, horns blowed, dogs barked and cats squalled, men yelled themselves hoarse, women and children screamed, and all other elements of discord went into a perfect jubilee of agonized excitement.*

The report went on to say that pistols and other deadly weapons were waved at the astonished expressmen. The *Richmond Telegram* reported that the little howitzer, the small cannon used on the Fourth of July, was fired in front of the courthouse.

Rocks were thrown and hoots, jeers and threats of violence came against the sheriff and the teamsters. The *Telegram* stated that "the notorious dead beat, Strickland" was conspicuously the leader of the belligerents. "Strickland loudly claimed to have sixty rounds of ammunition which would be used if anyone should try to escape the enclosure."

The men and teams from Richmond were kept within the courthouse fence until late in the afternoon. Attorney Peele obtained a restraining order from Judge Johnson. The order to stop the move came at three o'clock in the afternoon and was served to the officers. They were told to "git" and they "got," according to a later story. The men unloaded the wagons, returning the records to the courthouse, and were allowed to leave the fenced enclosure. As they left, they were followed through the town with shouting and threats from the crowd.

The behavior of the Centerville rioters caused a sensation around the county and was reported in state newspapers. On August 6, the *Indianapolis Weekly News* reported its opinion of the "Quaker Row":

> *Who, indeed, could have believed that the old, steady, quiet, intensely respectable community, largely mixed with Quakers of Wayne county would make a riot, form a mob, and not only indulge this phenomenal violence of temper, but do it in resistance of the law? Is this not incredible?*

The *Weekly News* went on to describe the battle between Centerville and Richmond. Centerville is given credit for being the longtime county seat, but the Indianapolis paper called it "a runt of town." Richmond's actions to have the county seat moved did not receive much sympathy either: "But Richmond was growing and selfish, and hoggish, in point of fact, and wanted the county business added to her iron and agricultural machine work to swell her importance."

The paper concluded the article by noting, "The little old town is victorious. But what will fat and saucy Richmond do? There is a smell of blood in the air."

Although the first round for removal was lost to Richmond, the battle was not over. Ten days later, Judge Johnson dissolved the restraining orders, stating that

> *the Judge of the Court possesses no Legislative powers, nor does he wish to assume the powers of a Board of County Commissioners…"To expound, not to make the law," is inscribed on the seal of the Circuit Court…the motion for the continuance of the restraining order heretofore granted by me, be and the same is hereby over-ruled.*

Preparations were made again for the wagons to go to Centerville. This time, they were met with three wagons owned by Centerville citizens, already loaded with records. In order to be prepared to stop any rioters, the two commissioners and three hundred men from Richmond came over by carriage and in four cars on a special train. Although the outcome was peaceful, they were prepared to protect the teamsters and help pack up the rest of the courthouse materials.

In 1914, a pioneer who witnessed the removal of the material from the old Centerville courthouse gave this recollection:

> *On that day when the old court house was abandoned, even the prisoners in the county jail being removed to Richmond under guard, the men, women and children of Centerville lined the streets and broke into a chorus of sobs as the last wagon moved east along the old National road and was lost to view in the dusk of a summer evening.*

The Richmond newspapers treated the final removal as a "sigh of relief" for the county. They congratulated the people of Centerville on their goodwill and stated that "the battle is now over." Events would soon show how mistaken their prediction was.

The first Richmond jail was constructed on the Courthouse Square. It was temporary housing for the prisoners until the larger jail was built. At the September 1873 meeting of the board of commissioners, the auditor was given orders to seek bids on a contract for a jail and sheriff's residence. In the same session, it was ordered that the jail part of the building in Centerville be taken down. The materials were to be carefully preserved and would be used in building the jail in Richmond. The commissioners purchased a 120-foot lot for the jail located on Green Street, extending north from Walnut and back to Jackson. They paid $1,800.

Commissioner Oliver Jones had not attended any of the meetings since the remonstrance from Centerville was rejected. If he could not stop the county seat move, he would not have any part in its removal. Jones chose not to run for the office in the fall.

William Peele, attorney for the Centerville faction, did not stop trying to get the county seat back for them. Although their case had been dismissed from the circuit court, Peele took an appeal to the Indiana Supreme Court and asked for another injunction and for the case to be heard before the court. This injunction was refused, but he persisted in trying to get a ruling from the court.

Work began on removing the jail in September 17. 1873. The workers were harassed and threatened, and work could not even get started. On September 26, the *Richmond Telegram* reported: "Alf Lashly of Centerville is luxuriating in jail, the result of the little unpleasantness at the above village on Tuesday. He refused to give bail, preferring to play martyr to the interests of Centerville, through the grates of a bastile. Let his name be recorded among the saints."

The commissioners issued an order to William Study, sheriff, to be at the site on September 22 and take whatever steps necessary to prevent an outbreak of violence. They emphatically stated, "We demand that you take such steps as will prevent such riotous assemblage and interference with the orders of said Board and interest of the county."

On September 19, Sheriff Study posted a notice to the people of Centerville, warning them to desist in carrying out any threats, concluding, "and while I sincerely hope that it will not be necessary to call upon me to protect the contractor and his workmen, IF NECESSARY, it will be my duty, and I shall perform it to the letter of the law."

The notice from the sheriff did not keep vandals from continuing to delay the workers. The *Richmond Times* reported that "the Centerville folks were on a Rampage again, having raised in a mob the other day to prevent their jail from being torn down by the Sheriff and parties."

There are no copies of Centerville newspapers of 1873, so Centerville's side of the controversy is not available. There is little doubt that some Centerville residents were as upset by the constant bickering and violence as others in the county. It is known, however, that several unruly malcontents continued to keep the anger going and caused a lot of trouble.

The case was soon before the Indiana Supreme Court. To further delay the work, another petition was circulated in Centerville asking to postpone any more work on the jail until the court decided the matter. The objectors

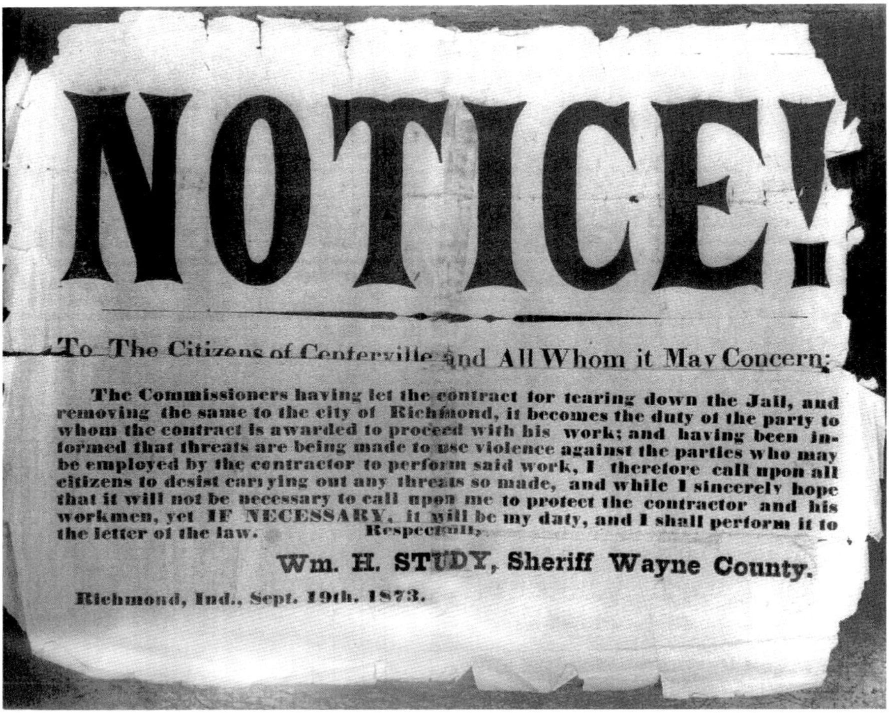

Sheriff's warning to Centerville, 1873. *Courtesy of Historic Centerville.*

promised that if the court would not grant a rehearing they would give up their fight and help with the work. On October 10, the Indiana Supreme Court affirmed the circuit court's decision, and all further attempts to stop the removal were finished. The case had been argued before three courts, and Centerville had no other place to appeal.

Judge Johnson, a resident of Cambridge City, stepped down on October 16, perhaps because had been drawn into the county seat controversy several times. When he resigned, he appointed Judge Holland to fill out the balance of his term or until the newly elected Judge Kibbey would take over the position.

CENTERVILLE'S LAST STAND

Work on taking down the jail was ordered to resume. Large derricks were raised to demolish the jail. As soon as they were in place, the vandals went to work. The first night, they cut the ropes into pieces. The second night, they sawed through the wooden structure. Armed men were sent to protect the workers.

On the night of October 28, seven guards were left in the sheriff's residence and jail over night to guard the tools of the workmen. Late in the evening, between 10:00 p.m. and 11:00 p.m., a group of fifty or sixty masked and armed men surrounded the building and demanded that the guards leave. The guards refused, and the mob began firing their guns into the building, breaking windows and filling the ceilings and walls with bullets. After an hour of the siege, three guards were able to escape and get a horse and buggy from a nearby stable. The men rushed to Richmond to raise the alarm.

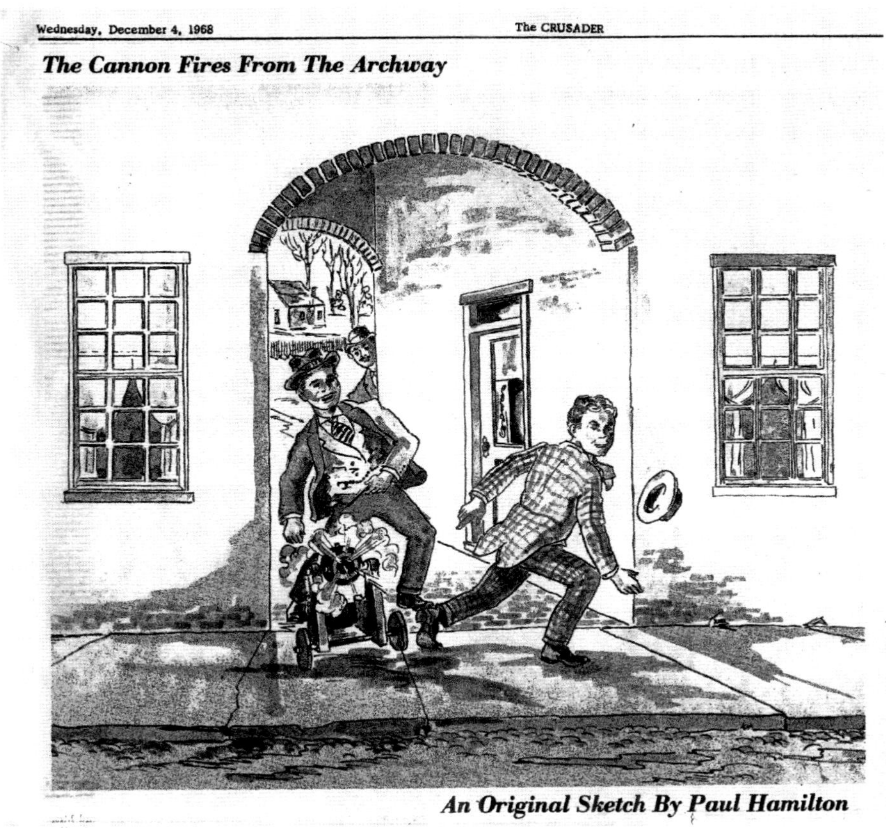

A cartoon by Centerville artist Paul Hamilton. *Courtesy of the* Crusader, *Centerville.*

Bells in the firehouse and courthouse were rung to rouse help in Richmond. At first, the people thought that there might be a fire. As soon as the word was passed, a posse of nearly one hundred men armed themselves and met at the railroad depot. A special train was made available; they were off to the rescue. Newspaper accounts noted that the train arrived in Centerville a little after 4:00 a.m.

The delay in the arrival of the posse had given the attackers time to do a lot of damage. When the remaining guards stubbornly refused to give up, the little cannon was placed facing the door of the sheriff's residence. They loaded it with scrap iron, old nails, bolts and other metal debris from a blacksmith shop. The cannon was then fired, shattering the heavy front door. A hail of bullets accompanied the cannon fire. The yelling mob rushed inside, and the four guards retreated to barricade themselves in the jail at the rear of the building.

The attackers demanded that the jail door be opened and gave the guards five minutes to open the door—or they would blow it open with the cannon. Recognizing that they were overpowered, the guards finally gave in. They were promised safety for themselves. To be sure they left town, the guards were escorted for about a mile down the road toward Richmond. They were told in no uncertain terms to "git."

When the posse arrived, all was quiet. A few stragglers were found on the street, but they appeared to be innocent and were not arrested. The guards had recognized Alfred Lashley among the attackers. He was questioned and eventually arrested for his part in the violence.

The cannon was discovered in a stable nearby. It was confiscated, and there were several stories told about what happened to it. One newspaper reported that the cannon was dragged through the muddy streets of Richmond and deposited in the new courthouse yard, "where it now frowns threateningly." Other stories tell of it being destroyed or sold. The little cannon was never again fired at any of the citizens of Wayne County or its buildings, and its current whereabouts are unknown.

In the afternoon after the last mob incident, thirty-five more men were sent to guard the house and jail. In the evening, several more volunteers came over, and the number grew to about seventy. They were armed with Spencer rifles and two hundred rounds of ammunitions. The commissioners had appealed to the governor for help, and he sent one thousand rounds of ammunition to be used if needed.

Fortunately, there was no more shooting. Several men were arrested who had instigated the riot. In the evening, a small crowd gathered across the street and carried on with some hooting and yelling. John Messick, who had charge of the "fort," informed the crowd that any movement toward the jail would be greeted with a volley of rifle fire and advised them to go about their own business. His warning was taken seriously, and no one made a move against the guards.

The next day after the riot, while the public buildings were still under guard, about two hundred men came with twenty wagons to remove the iron fence. The expensive $10,000 iron fence, also a point of contention, completely encircled the public square. In three hours, they had it taken down. A train with flatcars was sent over from Richmond. A total of sixteen cars moved the fence, which would be used at the new public square.

A large force of men worked to finish the job of razing the jail. There were no more incidents to delay it. The decision of the Supreme Court in favor of the commissioners put to rest any more ideas of challenging the county seat move. In an attempt to repair the damage to Centerville's reputation, and to be on better term with Richmond, this article was printed *Richmond Telegram* on November 28, 1873:

> *For some months past our town and county have been in such a state of excitement on the county-seat question...But now the storm has calmed down a little, the people outside of Centerville may wish to know how we have survived the shock of battle and the ravages of the late war...we would say that while we are conscious of having suffered wrong, we do not allow these things to disturb us in the honorable pursuits of life.*

Centerville could not cover up the sad events. The sheriff's records show that seven men were arrested on November 22. Alfred Lashley, William Hames, John Harvey, Hiram Strayer, Charles Wilson, Robert Commons and Fredrich Cappeller were charged with "Riot." They were indicted by the grand jury.

The "Wayne County Seat War" was reported in many state and national newspapers. The *Cincinnati Commercial* commented about Governor Hendricks sending help to quell the rioters. From July through November, the *Indianapolis Journal* published long articles discussing the events and giving opinions, pro and con, on the disgraceful affairs. The *New York Times* on

November 1, 1873, picked up an article from the *Cincinnati Times* describing at length the county seat war. Its headline reads: "HOT BLOOD IN INDIANA: THE COUNTY SEAT WAR IN WAYNE COUNTY—A JAIL ATTACKED BY DISGUISED ARMED MEN."

The war was over, but the bitterness lingered. Some Centerville people boycotted Richmond merchants. It was several years and generations later before the resentfulness finally faded away.

CHAPTER 11

RICHMOND'S FIRST COURTHOUSE

The business of the county proceeded in Richmond, with the usual affairs coming before the board of commissioners. The new Italianate-style courthouse was a simple, well-proportioned brick structure. The doors were topped by flat stone arches, and it had unadorned square-headed windows. It was covered with a low-pitched hipped roof with an open cupola. The cost for the construction was $22,700.

An 1884 map shows the National Road covered bridge. Not far from the old covered on South Second Street are the sheriff's residence and the first jail. The house had a tower, and the jail behind it shows a tall smokestack. Pictorial maps and fire insurance maps have verified locations of many buildings that have been torn down (and during which records were lost).

A new sheriff's residence and jail were built to replace the temporary one on the Courthouse Square. This was built on Second Street, one block west of the courthouse.

THE LAST SAD ACT

In 1886, the jail and the courthouse became the center of another dramatic event, the last hanging in Wayne County. This event caused Indiana legislators to change Indiana law regarding how capital punishment was carried out.

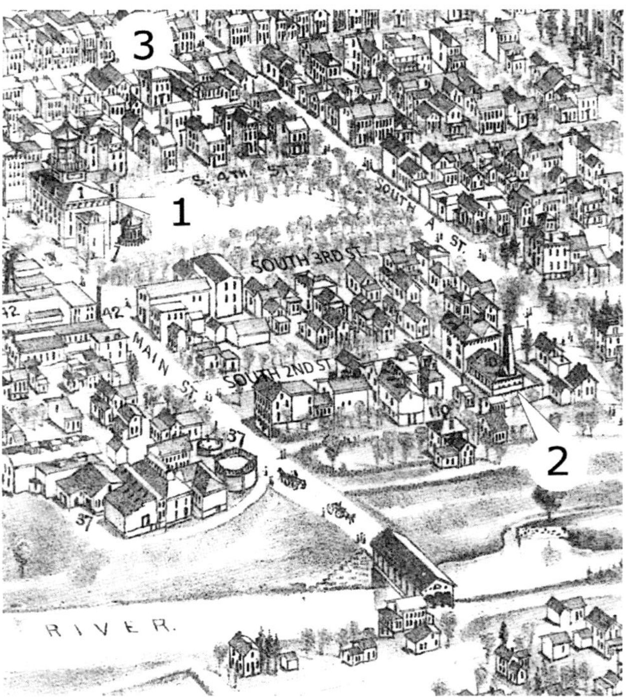

Above: Richmond's first courthouse, built in 1873. *Courtesy of Wayne County Historical Museum.*

Left: A pictorial map of Richmond, 1884, showing location of (1) the first courthouse, (2) the county jail and (3) the log courthouse. *Map by Gunty Atkins.*

On a sleepy March afternoon in Hagerstown, the town marshal, Tom Murray, was loafing in front of Shively's hardware store. He looked up to see Still Bates coming up to him.

"Tom, come here a minute, I want to see you," Bates called, showing no signs of distress.

Murray walked over to Bates and asked what he wanted.

"I guess you'll have to take me to Richmond."

"What for?" Murray asked.

"I have killed my wife!"

Murray could not believe what he was hearing. Noticing the blood on Bates's clothing, he knew that he was telling the truth. He handcuffed Bates, took him to the engine house and locked him in an iron cage that served as the town's jail. When Murray searched him, he found the bloody knife. Bates had cut his estranged wife's throat after an argument.

In 1886, it was not uncommon for lynchings to occur in Indiana. Word soon spread in Hagerstown, and Murray hurried Bates to the railroad station. A crowd gathered at the station, many having visited the crime scene. They were in a lynching mood. Murray wanted no part of this unlawful act. He drew his gun and told the crowd that it was his duty to get the prisoner to the county jail in Richmond.

When the train arrived, Murray slipped Bates out a side door and onto the train. He posted armed guards at both ends of the car to hold off the shouting crowd. The train pulled away and stopped at Washington (Greens Fork) to take on Deputy Sheriff Charles Murray, brother of Tom. They soon arrived in Richmond, and Bates was put in jail there.

Nathaniel "Still" Bates was twenty-six years old. He had married Catherine "Kitty" Hoover seven years before. Bates had a reputation for being a mean drunk and was abusive to his wife. She, with her two young daughters, had run away from him when they lived in Council Bluffs, Iowa. They came to Indiana to live with her mother. Kitty had a hard time supporting her family. Sometimes her brother, Tom Hoover, who also lived in Hagerstown, helped the family.

Bates did not know where Kitty was living until Tom wrote to him in Council Bluffs. He told Bates to come take care of his family, as he, Tom, was tired of helping. Bates arrived on the train in Hagerstown on Christmas Eve 1885 and was reluctantly allowed to stay with Kitty, the girls and her mother.

The sheriff's residence and Wayne County Jail, 1873. *Courtesy of Wayne County Historical Museum.*

Kitty refused to go back to Bates as his wife. He caught her alone on that March day when he came back to town from a day's work on a farm. He tried to get Kitty to agree to come back to him, but she refused again. This time, he became angry and violent. He struck her down and cut her throat with his freshly sharpened knife. Instantly regretting what he had done, he went to the town pump to wash off a bit and went in search of the town marshal.

Nathaniel Bates was charged with murder and pleaded guilty. Curious men and boys attended the jury trial, many having to stand outside for lack of room. Women usually did not attend trials unless they were somehow involved. It took only two hours for the jury to decide, since Bates had confessed his guilt. The courthouse bell was rung, indicating that the jury had reached a guilty verdict. The *Richmond Telegram* reported that at the ringing of the courthouse bell "men and boys rushed pell mell in the direction of the court house as though they were going to a fire."

Bates was sentenced to hang on August 26, 1886. Hagerstown was greatly upset over the murder. The newspapers in Richmond, in the county and around the state were full of lengthy stories. They described gruesome details

Nathaniel Bates. *Courtesy of Wayne County Historical Museum.*

of the crime, the trial and the hanging. The execution was to be done behind the sheriff's residence in the exercise yard between the house and the jail.

Bates asked to have his picture taken before the hanging. He did not like the one that had been printed in the paper when he was arrested. Sheriff Isaac Gorman's wife felt sorry for Bates and sent a chair, shawl and bronze ornament for the picture.

On the same day, Bates received a visit from his two daughters, seven and four. Their grandmother Hoover had brought them over for the only time they had seen him since the murder. A picture was taken of the children with their father.

The hanging gallows was erected in the same area where the pictures were taken. On the Sunday before the hanging, an immense crowd came for a look at Bates. The streets around the jail were jammed, and 653 people were allowed, 20 at a time, to pass by Bates's cell. Finally, a strong thunderstorm drove the crowd away.

On the day of the hanging, the streets filled as though it were a holiday celebration. Streams of horse-drawn vehicles came on the turnpikes. Morning trains arrived with cars loaded with people from far and near. Hundreds of people filled Richmond for this third public hanging in Wayne County.

Passes were given out to 150 official witnesses to view the execution. About 100 men entered the execution site, which was enclosed with brick walls. Tom Murray, the arresting officer, chose not to attend. At 12:30 p.m., Sheriff Gorman sprung the trap, and Nathaniel Bates paid the ultimate price for his act of murder.

The horrible show was not over. People were allowed to come into the jail a short time later to look at Bates in his coffin. It was reported that 4,300 people viewed Bates's body in the jail. Hundreds more went to the funeral home for a look. The following day, a funeral was held at St. Mary's Catholic Church. The *Telegram* again reported that the church was packed with standing room only and that many could not get in. Finally, Bates was laid to rest in Council Bluffs after another elaborate funeral in that place.

The behavior of the crowds and the newspaper publicity so disgusted and distressed the people involved that they wanted to do something about the Indiana law. Sheriff Gorman appealed to Henry U. Johnson, state senator, proposing ideas for new legislation concerning how executions should be handled in Indiana.

Senator Johnson agreed with Gorman. He introduced a bill to amend Section 128 of the Criminal Code. Senate Bill Number 126, an Act Concerning the Death Penalty, was introduced in January 1887. While many in the legislature agreed with this change, it was not brought to a vote because of legislative infighting. The session of the legislature closed with very little being accomplished.

The Indiana legislature only met every other year. This amendment was one of the first bills to be passed when the legislature met in 1889. The act would move all executions from county jails to the state prison. Credit for getting this law changed is due to the persistent efforts by Wayne County legislators.

Sadly, because it took two years to pass the bill, there were two more public hangings in Indiana with the same type of ghoulish behavior by crowds who thronged to watch.

All three of the Wayne County seats had one hanging. Each execution was strongly opposed by religious groups, primarily the Quakers. Capital punishment is still debated in every state in the United States. Because of the continued pressure of Wayne County legislators in 1889, no more such public spectacles were carried out in Indiana's counties. The whole unfortunate process is handled with dignity, and every opportunity for leniency is given before the act is completed.

CHAPTER 12

WAYNE COUNTY'S SIXTH COURTHOUSE

By the late 1880s, it was obvious to the commissioners that the 1873 courthouse was not large enough for all the county business. The building had been constructed rapidly in less than six months. It was not much larger than the last one in Centerville. Records for the county had grown so much that there were concerns for their safekeeping. Other spaces had to be rented to store them. Offices were crowded, and more space was needed. An attempt to remodel or build on to the first Richmond courthouse would be very expensive and still not satisfy the need for a newer, more modern facility.

Interest in a new courthouse was discussed throughout the county and particularly in Richmond. In an article for the *Richmond Evening Item* on March 28, 1889, a reporter talked to leading citizens and business owners in the county to hear their ideas on the subject. The reporter was surprised to find that almost everyone he spoke to wanted a new courthouse as soon as possible.

John Dougan, capitalist and cashier of the Second National Bank, said, "We have got to do it soon, and the sooner it is done the better; building material is cheap and so is labor…Our county pride I think, requires that we have a new court house, and the commissioners ought to order it at once."

Ed Morris, book dealer stated, "I think that it is…a matter of public improvement and would be a benefit to the city and county."

Tom Nicholson, book dealer and printer agreed: "I am decidedly in favor of a new court house. Some time ago a gentleman was visiting our city and he said he would look at our courthouse and I was ashamed for him to see it and asked him not to go. It's a disgrace to the county. We ought to have had it built twelve years ago."

A few voices spoke up against it, like Barney Flemming, cigar dealer. "I would rather see pikes bought and have a race track and a fair"—he was speaking of the county buying up the toll roads.

The reporter traveled out into the county and found mostly agreement that the old courthouse had long outlived its usefulness and needed to be replaced. With public sentiment generally in agreement, plans were made by the commissioners to build a newer, larger courthouse. In June 1889, an order was made to construct a new courthouse on the south side of public square beside the current one. The reason for building was to be "located in order to provide offices for officers and Courts and a safe and secure place to store and preserve records."

A remonstrance was filed against building a new courthouse in September, but the commissioners rejected it. Wayne County had been through this before. All of the previous court decisions agreed that the board of commissioners in the county had the final say about the county seat headquarters.

The three commissioners—John Bowman, Mark Maudlin and Daniel K. Zeller—made trips to Pittsburgh, Indianapolis, Terre Haute, Lafayette and Muncie to look at plans and other courthouses.

In November 1889, James McLaughlin, architect from Cincinnati, was employed to prepare design plans and specifications. The cost of the construction was estimated at $260,000. The commissioners traveled to Cincinnati to look over McLaughlin's ideas. The plans were approved in December 1889. John Macy was elected commissioner, replacing John Bowman, in 1890. He served on the board of commissioners with Maudlin and Zeller while the courthouse was being built.

The style chosen for the architecture of the building was Romanesque Revival, a style popularized by Henry H. Richardson. He was a graduate of Harvard and a student at the École des Beaux-Arts in Paris from 1860 to 1862. His designs emphasized wall-bearing systems, horizontal lines and rounded arches as opposed to the pointed arches of the Gothic style. He liked to use masses of stone with many windows to light the interior. This was considered a dignified style for public buildings.

Richardson had designed several buildings in the East, and his style and designs were copied by other leading architects of the time. Romanesque Revival buildings are found in many U.S. cities. Richardson is often given the title of "father of modern architecture" in the United States.

Other buildings of this style were built in Richmond about the same time as the courthouse. The first Richmond City Building, the original Morrison-Reeves Library and the old firehouse on North Eighth Street all had many similar features. John Hasecoster, a well-known Richmond architect, designed them.

Aaron G. Campfield of Richmond was awarded the general contract to build the new building in April 1890. William H. and Edwin M. Campfield worked with him. The contract called for Campfield to oversee all of the building construction except for the electrical installation. William S. Kaufman was the superintendent for the courthouse construction. He had been in charge of other large building projects in Wayne County and had a reputation for capable work.

The commissioners approved all of the best building materials and up-to-date improvements. The building was to be built on the south side of the county square, facing east. It would be three stories high and have electric lighting, a large sewer system, steam heat and an elevator for public use.

The project would be quite expensive. The state law allowed only a certain percentage of tax money to be used for the construction. In order to raise the rest of the money, the first $150,000 issue of bonds was sold in June 1890. They were all sold to Daniel Reid for a 4.5 percent interest rate, issued for ten years.

Mr. Reid was interviewed in the *Richmond Evening Item* in an 1889 article for his opinion about a new courthouse: "I am in favor of a new court house, and would like to see it built, and don't care how soon it is done. The one we now have is not suitable for this county."

Daniel Reid's occupation was listed as teller at the Second National Bank. He also may have been an officer of the bank. Reed became very wealthy and helped Richmond obtain other fine buildings. He paid for the Reid Memorial Presbyterian Church and the original Reid Hospital building. These were built a few years later. It is mystery how he was able to finance all of the bonds offered for sale by the county.

The work proceeded, and many local men were given employment. A huge basement and trenches were dug for the foundation. Stone and cement

Richmond's two courthouses side by side. *Courtesy of Wayne County Historical Musuem.*

A view of Richmond 1893, with (1) first Richmond courthouse, (2) second Richmond courthouse and (3) sheriff's residence and jail. *Courtesy of Morrison-Reeves Library.*

United States of America

NUMBER 216 — STATE OF INDIANA. — $1000 — SERIES II

Wayne County

COURT HOUSE BOND.

The County of Wayne in the State of Indiana will pay to the bearer sixteen years from the date hereof the sum of ONE THOUSAND DOLLARS, in lawful money of the United States of America together with interest thereon at the rate of five per cent per annum payable semi annually on the first days of January and July in each year as evidenced by and upon the presentation and surrender of the annexed interest coupons as they respectively mature.

Both principal and interest of this Bond are hereby made payable at the American Exchange National Bank in the City and State of New York.

This Bond is one of a series of twenty five of the same date tenor and amount issued for the purpose of constructing a Court House for said County in compliance with the order of the Board of Commissioners thereof duly entered of record and in full conformity with Chapter 7º of the Acts of the General Assembly of the State of Indiana of 1891.

And it is hereby certified and recited that all acts conditions and things required to be done precedent to and in the issuing of said bonds have been properly done happened and been performed in regular and due form as required by law and that the total indebtedness of said County including this series of bonds does not exceed the statutory or constitutional limitations.

In Witness Whereof, the Board of Commissioners have hereunto signed their names and caused the Auditor of said County to attach his certificate hereto together with his signature and the Seal of said Board this first day of July 1891.

STATE OF INDIANA, WAYNE COUNTY, SS.

Commissioners of Wayne County.

J. Finley Newlin County Auditor do certify that the annexed Bond was issued to the County Treasurer this first day of July 1891.

In Testimony Whereof I have hereunto set my hand and affixed the Seal of said Board of County Commissioners this first day of July 1891.

Attest

Auditor Wayne County Indiana.

A $1,000 bond for the 1893 courthouse. It shows the original gold commissioners' seal. *Photo by Edward Lafever.*

formed the foundation. Three million bricks were used on the thick interior walls, which required a large force of bricklayers.

Limestone from Bedford, Indiana, was ordered for the exterior walls. Six hundred wagonloads of stone were hauled from the train station to the building site. The limestone facings were cut on the site by 125 stonecutters. As each floor was completed, steam-powered hoists were moved to the next floor to lift up the huge stone blocks.

A second series of bonds for $125,000 was issued in June 1891. Again the whole amount was sold to Daniel Reid for fourteen years at 5 percent interest.

By January 1992, work moved forward on the interior. Most of the outside was complete, with the exception of a few details. Mr. Campfield was given extra payment for carving the county seal over the north entrance.

The early commissioners' books showed that a county seal was ordered and paid for in 1819. It was a surprise to the current commissioners because no one had seen the Wayne County seal for a long time. A search was made to locate something to prove that it really had been used. Nothing was found until the book containing the courthouse bonds, sold to Daniel Reid, was discovered. The bond book was several inches think, weighing about twenty pounds and stored on a top of the tall shelves full of the commissioners' records.

In 1993, when the courthouse was cleaned, the carved seal was photographed for the newspaper. It had not been lost, just overlooked for a long time. Although a new courthouse logo has been designed, the seal has served as a symbol for the county for 191 years.

The finest materials were selected for the interior. Marble wainscoting was laid along the bottom of the walls. Twelve polished columns, twenty feet in height and twenty inches in diameter, were made of polished Concord granite from New Hampshire. A magnificent staircase rises from the first floor. The stairs are of white marble, with the banisters and handrails of polished granite.

Construction of the courthouse proceeded as well as could be expected. The newspapers reported that a strike and bad weather caused some delays. Furnishings began to arrive in early 1893. Fine oak furniture and other wooden decorations in the Romanesque style were ordered from Ohmer Brothers of Dayton, Ohio.

The Fenton Metallic Manufacturing Company of Jamestown, New York, was given the contract for all the metal furnishings, such as vaults and shelving.

A carving of the original county seal—a tree, plow and sheaf of wheat. Ordered in 1819. Located over the north door of the 1893 courthouse. *Photo by Edward Lafever.*

In October 1892, the commissioners received a letter from W.H. Bennett of the Fenton Company, causing a delay in setting up the offices: "We regret to say that our entire factory burned down on the 20th [October]…and the fire completely destroyed the entire work for the Richmond court house, which was very nearly completed and could have been shipped out in ten days."

Despite the delays, the courthouse was finished and had a final inspection by outside inspectors. It was approved, and the commissioners accepted it on February 25, 1893. The magnificent new courthouse was ready for everyone to see.

The public was invited to an open house on March 20, 1893. Patriotic bunting was hung in the treasurer's office. Everything was clean, shiny and polished. Electric lights brightened the rooms. Wayne County had built one of the most impressive courthouses in Indiana. The public was allowed to go through and inspect the building for the next month.

Reporters who passed through on the first day gave glowing descriptions of the building. The *Richmond Evening Item* reported:

The new Wayne County Courthouse, circa 1893, enclosed with an iron fence. *Courtesy of Wayne County Historical Museum.*

> *Hundreds of visitors wended their way through the broad and stately halls of Wayne's new temple of justice today. The public generally was invited, and for the next month the big building will have the close inspection of the citizens of the entire county...It is doubtful if Treasurer Cook will recognize his office when he comes home, the comparison between the old dingy room and the new quarters being so great.*

The whole building was lighted with electric lights—"nearly one thousand incandescent lamps are distributed among the offices." Gaslight fixtures had also been installed as a backup for electricity, which was not always reliable. Gas fireplaces were placed in several of the offices.

No large project is without its critics. There had been complaints that the building was much too large and that there would never be enough county business to fill it. It was true for a few years.

The county assessor, surveyor, clerk, treasurer, commissioners, the county school superintendent and others conducting county business had spacious offices. Rooms were available for rent to lawyers. The Wayne County Horticultural Society was given space. The Wayne County Historical Society

Patriotic banners in the treasurer's office for the grand opening. *From the 1893* Wayne County Atlas.

"has compartments which will enable them to have a permanent place for the collection of valuable relics."

Several decorations adorned the new building. A dome-shaped ceiling was beautifully frescoed and ornamented by artist Charles E. Chapman of Chicago. He was also contracted to fresco and decorate sheriff's, recorder's, auditor's, commissions, treasurer's and clerk's offices and two courtrooms, as well as all corridors and ceilings that are plastered for frescoing. His work cost $5,000. These beautiful frescos and much of the decoration were covered up years later as the building was remodeled for heat conservation and a changing of the office spaces.

In September 1892, a Soldiers' Memorial was ordered at a cost of $1,700. It was designed by architect McLaughlin. The large marble tablet with a patriotic inscription is mounted under a large bronze eagle. Solomon Meredith, major general, veteran of the Civil War, furnished the inscription for the marble tablet: "Their trade was not war but peace; They waged war that peace might come; The union they preserved in peace. A grateful people holds them in sacred remembrance."

The clerk's office. *From the 1893* Wayne County Atlas.

Some of the other original decorations are still in place. Carvings on the wooden railings in the circuit courtroom on the third-floor banisters are original. This is the oldest original courtroom in the building. Original marble corner sinks are still in use in some of the offices. The gas fireplaces were closed off because they lost too much heat. Some can still be seen, and others have been covered. A statue of Oliver Morton was placed in the upper hall.

The heating system for the massive courthouse was a large expense for the county. Steam pipes were installed throughout the three floors. At first, the plan was to heat with natural gas. In November 1892, the Richmond Natural Gas Company requested that service to the courthouse be discontinued due to a large increase in the number of domestic customers.

In December 1892, a new oil plant was ordered to be installed. Crude oil would be used to fire the large furnace to produce steam heat. In January 1893, the *Richmond Palladium* predicted a bad outcome for this type of heat:

An original marble sink, from 1893. It is still in use. *Photo by Edward Lafever.*

> *The county commissioners seem to have an elephant on their hands in our grand new Norman-Gothic court house. It is so big the commissioners can't get blankets enough to keep it warm, so when the gas failed they conducted to try oil, and this experiment is likely to fail.*
>
> *After spending a very considerable sum of money in an oil plant they bought a car load of oil at the expense of $130; this lasted in heating the edifice just seven days—almost twenty dollars a day for oil alone.*

The heating fuel was changed to a coal-fired furnace in less than twenty years. In February 1912, the *Exponent* of Hagerstown printed this complaint: "Few of the citizens of Wayne County know or realize the cost of heating the Court house at Richmond, the county capital. During zero weather and even ten degrees above, the large furnace that heats the steam boiler consumes three tons of coal a day."

Heating the courthouse continued to be expensive, and several changes were made to cut down the heat loss. Ceilings were lowered, which covered up the painted ceilings. Gas fireplaces were covered and chimneys were closed. As energy has become more expensive, efforts are still ongoing to make the system more efficient.

Other conveniences were added to the building. An elevator was installed to run from the basement to the attic. It was first powered by hydraulic water

A group of county officials in front of the first Richmond courthouse, 1891. *Courtesy of Wayne County Historical Museum.*

power. Some years later, it was changed to electricity. For many years, people were taken up and down in the elevator by an operator before it became self-operating. Tom Murray, the Hagerstown town marshal who arrested Nathaniel Bates for murder in 1886, served as the elevator operator in the courthouse for many years.

The first Richmond courthouse was not needed after the move into the new one. The old building was put up for sale at auction on April 1, 1893, shortly after the grand open house in March. It was purchased by James M. Starr for $330.00. Other property, including the courthouse furnishings, sold for a total of $1,059.30.

The bell from the open cupola atop the old courthouse was bought by J.F. Davenport. E.M. Haas, who wrote articles for the Richmond newspaper, related what he believed to be the history of the courthouse bell. The bell had been used at the fire department on South Fifth Street. When this location was abandoned, the bell went to the old city building. It was transferred to the courthouse, where it notified citizens of the convening of the court. It rang in 1886 to tell the spectators that the jury had come back from deliberating the fate of Nathaniel Bates.

When Mr. Davenport purchased the bell, he sold it to Dr. Holterman of New Paris. According to Haas, the bell was buried and covered over with earth. Only one person knew where the bell was located at the time of his writing. Haas was interested in recovering the bell and giving it to the Wayne County Historical Museum.

There is now a bell on the museum grounds. The history of the bell was lost, and only vague rumors were known about where it came from. The information about the old courthouse bell indicates that this might be the same bell that hung in the cupola of Richmond's first courthouse for almost twenty years.

The county commissioners were sensitive to complaints about the expense for the new courthouse. They looked for ways to cut costs. In March 1893, according the *Wayne Farmer* at Hagerstown, the commissioners refused to pay for telephones used by the county officers.

The wars for the Wayne County Courthouse and the location of the county seat were over. The fine new courthouse became old and passed its 100th birthday in 1993. The predictions that it was too big and would never be filled were wrong.

Over those one hundred years, many changes took place in the county. Two world wars and an economic depression came and went. A surge of financial growth came in the 1950s; Wayne County was prosperous with expanding manufacturing and flourishing farms. Richmond and the county towns expanded with new housing additions, and populations grew.

Courthouse business increased over the years, continuing to change its nature or be eliminated. The county school superintendent was no longer needed when the county schools consolidated in the 1960s. Toll roads were purchased in the 1890s, and the road department has continued to improve its 765 miles of roads. The Horticultural Society ended. The Purdue Extension office takes care of 4-H and other related activities. The historical society collection is now located at the Wayne County Historical Museum on North A Street in Richmond.

Wayne County is known for having some of the best-cared-for roads in Indiana. When the first rural mail deliveries came to Wayne County as a pilot program in the late 1890s, the postal inspector commented that he had never seen finer roads for the postal carriers to travel.

Wayne County closed the county poorhouse. A welfare department and county clinic now provide help to those in need. A large portion of county taxes goes to social services.

In 1976, plans were made for a county administration building to be built across Third Street, east of the courthouse. This office annex was opened in 1978. It has two stories. The basement was constructed as a facility for civil defense and as a combined radio communications center for all law enforcement and civil defense. There are other offices in the basement and on the first floor. The clerk's office, judges' chambers and courtrooms are still located in the courthouse.

In anticipation of the 100th birthday of the courthouse, the current commissioners had the stonework carefully cleaned and repaired where needed. A new roof was put on in 1991. The cost of the stonework was $235,000, and the roof cost $700,000.

The work on the courthouse was completed by Oberle & Associates of Richmond and guided by Dave Novak, project engineer for the firm of Odle, McGuire and Shook of Indianapolis. Mr. Novak spoke to Historic

The Wayne County administration office annex. *Photo by Edward Lafever.*

The Wayne County Courthouse, 2010. *Photo by Edward Lafever.*

Centerville about the work in 1992. He stated that the 1893 building "is in outstanding condition for its age." He also said that it was one of his favorites of all the courthouses he had visited in Indiana.

The first sheriff's residence and jail was used until a second jail was built in 1959. The old house and jail were sold at auction on October 22, 1959, to John Graf. The new facility was built on the south side of the block between Second and Third Streets and South A Street across from the courthouse. The building that housed the jail was called the Wayne County Safety Building. In 1959, the commissioners' records show that women housed in the women's prison on South Tenth Street would be moved to the Wayne County Safety Building. The women's prison had been built in 1906 at the Home of Friendless Women.

The last jail and law enforcement office was completed in 2004. This latest addition to county buildings covers the whole block between Second and Third Streets and from Main Street to North A Street. It is located diagonally across the street from the courthouse on the site of the old Swain Robinson factory.

After the September 11, 2001 attack on the Twin Towers of the World Trade Center in New York, measures for protecting the courthouse were put into place. Large decorative flowerpots were placed in front of the main entrance, and a security screening unit was fitted just inside. Security guards check everyone who comes in. This need for protection has taken away some of the grandeur of the beautiful marble staircase and the tall pillars.

Every effort is being made to make county buildings more energy efficient. The newer buildings have been built with energy-conserving insulation and heating and cooling systems. Taking care of the buildings and wise use of tax money will continue to be a challenge. Wayne County has honored and preserved the historic 1893 courthouse while continuing to build new buildings for the future.

CHAPTER 13

HISTORICAL TIDBITS

While searching old records and looking at old maps, other interesting things about the Wayne County courthouses turned up. It was known by some historians that the first log courthouse had been put up as a house in Richmond. It was located at 38 South Front Street (now Fifth Street), little more than a block from the first and second Richmond courthouses.

In 1952, the log courthouse, covered with clapboard and divided into two apartments, was rediscovered. The lot had been sold, and the old house was to be razed to make a parking lot. As the huge, hewed logs were uncovered, it was identified by several as Wayne County's first courthouse.

There was a call to move it and restore it from people interested in preservation. Suggestions were made to move it to the Wayne County Historical Museum on North A Street, but citizens of Centerville were the ones who came to its rescue. The Centerville Lions Club led the campaign to raise funds to save the building. In 1954, the log courthouse was moved and restored on the Wayne County fairgrounds in Centerville, now the Centerville High School campus.

When a tornado ripped through the Centerville fairgrounds in March 1976, several of the fair buildings were badly damaged. Fortunately, the log courthouse was spared. Land for a larger fairground had been purchased in 1975 on Salisbury Road, west of Richmond. Plans for the new fairgrounds went into high gear. The 1976 fair, although in temporary housing, was held at the new Salisbury Road location.

As the Centerville fairgrounds were cleared, the question of what to do with the log courthouse was raised again. The old building was taken down and the logs carefully stored. Historic Centerville, Inc., had purchased the historic Mansion House on Main Street in Centerville. The society took over the project of once again saving the log courthouse.

The Mansion House was built in 1840 as a stagecoach stop and as an inn and hotel along the National Road. It was a popular place for politicians, travelers and salesmen to stay in while visiting Centerville. The lot on which the Mansion House stands is large, and there was space on the west side of the property for the log courthouse. It took a few years for funds to be raised to restore the log building. During that time, a search was conducted to find hewed logs from other log buildings to replace the deteriorated ones. Although some logs have been replaced, the building contains about 80 percent of its original materials. The restoration of the log courthouse was completed on the Mansion House property in 1997.

An astonishing discovery showed up when the Richmond Sanborn Fire Insurance Map of 1891 was examined. The location of the first and second courthouses, along with that of the log courthouse and the first Richmond

The restored Salisbury log courthouse and Mansion House. *Photo by Edward Lafever.*

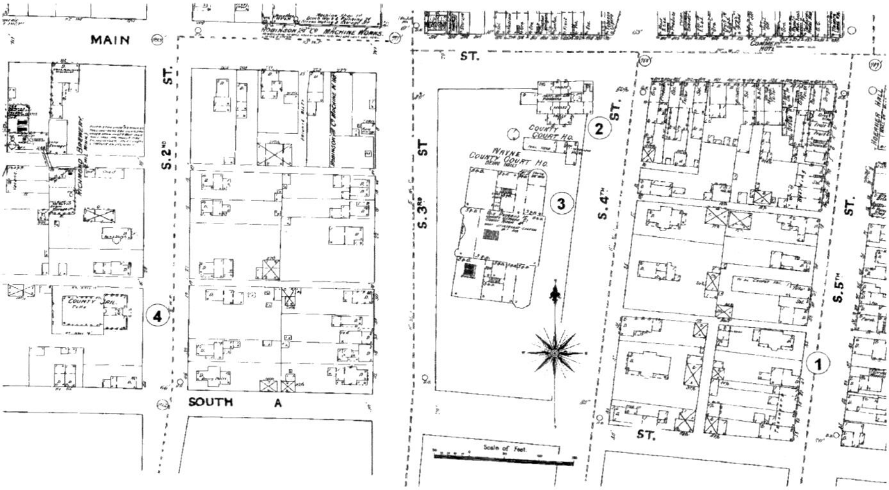

Richmond Sanborn map, 1891. 1) old log courthouse; 2) first Richmond courthouse; and 3) 1893 courthouse. *Map by Gunty Atkins.*

jail, are shown. For a couple of years, three out of the six Wayne County courthouses stood within a block of one another. The map here shows how the present courthouse dwarfs the first one sitting next to it.

Although the first county seat, Salisbury, was lost to history, the log courthouse was not forgotten. In 1897, George Julian spoke of it in a speech at the Old Settlers' Picnic. He purposely went to see if it was still located where it had been moved. The same information was stated by E.M. Haas in his *History of Early County Courthouses* about 1935. In 1941, the old building's location was mentioned again in a newspaper article.

This information helped to establish the truth about the first Wayne County courthouse.

Is that a Castle?

One can understand the concern and amazement of Wayne County citizens when they first saw the last courthouse, a huge castle-like building. No expense had been spared with its ornamented, frescoed walls and marble columns and floors. County residents had been accustomed to the smaller, cramped quarters of the old brick courthouse. It would appear that such a large building would never be needed and would be hard to keep up.

The critics had a point about the expense, but they were wrong about the space not being needed. The careful planning and thought by the 1893 commissioners resulted in a county courthouse that has stood for nearly 120 years.

CENTERVILLE COURTHOUSE AND JAIL

When Richmond won the battle for the county seat, the courthouse in Centerville was of no more use as a public building. The people of Richmond raised the funds to pay the county $80,000 for all the public property in Centerville. The fourth courthouse, Centerville's second, was sold by the county in 1873. It stood on the northeast corner of Main and Cross Streets (renamed Morton Street).

The last Centerville courthouse, circa 1880s. It was destroyed by fire in 1915. *Courtesy of the author.*

The Centerville Center Township Public Library. *Photo by Edward Lafever.*

For the first few years, the building was owned by the Hoosier Organ Company. The old cupola was removed because it served no purpose and was expensive to maintain. The cupola once held the bell to call the townspeople together for the court. The post office was two doors to the east. In 1915, a fire ravaged the old building and several of the wooden buildings on either side. The burned area was cleared, and new buildings took their place. This was the last remnant of Centerville's county seat history.

The Centerville sheriff's residence, built for $80,000, was sold to Simon and Flora McConaha for $1,250. In 1924, it became the home of the Masonic Lodge. The building was purchased in 1997 by the Centerville Library. The building was beautifully remodeled and became the Centerville Center Township Public Library, dedicated in 1999.

They Served the County Well

In every story there are notable characters who stand out. Many men and women took part in the founding and growth of Wayne County. They suffered through hardship in the War of 1812 and the Civil War. They battled for their towns to have prominence in the county and for its symbol, the courthouse. Sometimes they won; sometimes they lost.

Struggles make people stronger, which in turn builds strong leaders. This leadership has its examples in notable men who lived in the nineteenth-century history of Wayne County.

Richard Rue, Joseph Holman and Isaac Julian were leaders in Wayne County's early founding. Each one played a part to keep slavery out and make Wayne County's influence felt in the Indiana legislature.

THE JULIAN FAMILY

Isaac Julian's three sons carried on his example of leadership in spite of losing their father at an early age. Jacob Julian (1815–1910) became a prominent lawyer in Centerville. Jacob and George were law partners until political views caused them to separate. Jacob and his son, John, worked together until he moved to Indianapolis. Jacob and his neighbor, Sylvester Johnson, purchased land east of Indianapolis in 1871. They divided it into lots and named it Irvington. Jacob was a distinguished judge in the courts of Indiana.

George Julian (1817–1899) practiced law as his profession. He was elected to the Indiana legislature in 1845 and again in 1849 to serve as a representative to Congress. His political career in Congress ended in 1871.

George was passionate about seeing justice and freedom for slaves. He worked tirelessly against slavery and capital punishment. He fought for black and women's equality and suffrage and the cause for temperance. Along the way, he changed political parties, going from Whig to Free-Soil to Republican to finally associating himself with the Democrat Party. Julian never backed down from a fight that he felt was for the good of the country.

The ongoing battle to move the county seat from Centerville caused the Julian family much distress. Sensing the end of Centerville's domination in the county, George purchased property from Jacob and moved to Irvington in 1873.

The youngest Julian brother, Isaac (1823–1910), had interests in history and literature. He studied law and practiced for a time but decided that he did not like it for a profession. Instead, Isaac developed his writing skills by composing poetry and essays for newspapers and magazines of the day. He was intensely interested in antislavery and humanitarian phases of politics. In 1858, Isaac bought the Centerville newspaper, the *True Republican*, for which he was both editor and publisher. In 1864, he purchased a Richmond newspaper. The two newspapers were merged and became the *Indiana Radical*. The name was changed to *Julian's Radical* as his opinions moved away from the Republican Party.

Isaac went heavily into debt with his newspaper business. In 1872, he was forced to stop publishing the *Radical*. The closing of the newspaper and the brothers' moving out of town closed the era of the Julian family's influence in Wayne County.

Governor Oliver P. Morton

Oliver Morton (1823–1877), Indiana's Civil War governor, spent his early life in the Centerville community. He practiced law there until he became governor in 1861. Morton was elected again in 1864. In the summer of 1865, Morton suffered a stroke, which affected his lower body. He never walked again without the assistance of a cane.

Morton traveled to consult doctors in Europe. Their treatments did not totally restore him, but he was able to take up his duties and complete his term of office. In 1867, he was elected to the Senate of the United States. Morton continued to serve in that capacity until his death in 1877.

Morton was a friend and supporter of Abraham Lincoln. His first political affiliation was with the Democrat Party. His views conflicted with the party over slavery, and he became a Republican, attending its organizational convention as a delegate. Although he never returned to live in Wayne County after serving as governor, he is honored by the county with a life-size statue in the courthouse.

Solomon Meredith

Solomon Meredith (1810–1875) came to Wayne County when he was nineteen. At age twenty-four, he was elected sheriff, serving two terms. He served four terms in the state legislature and was appointed to the post of U.S. marshal in 1849. At the beginning of the Civil War, Governor Morton appointed Meredith to lead the Nineteenth Indiana. His initial rank was colonel, but he rose to the rank of brigadier general. He was given command of the "Iron Brigade" from November 1862 to July 1863. The brigade was made up of two Indiana, one Michigan and three Wisconsin regiments. While leading troops in the Battle of Gettysburg, Meredith was severely wounded. He served in several other capacities until the end of the war.

Meredith served as surveyor general of the Montana Territory from 1867 to 1869. He returned to his farm, Oakland, near Cambridge City and ended his days there.

NEIGHBORS BUT NOT FRIENDS

The lives of George Julian, Solomon Meredith and Oliver Morton intertwined in Wayne County and in Washington. All three were involved in Indiana politics as well as on the national scene. Although from similar backgrounds, their political views differed greatly on some of the most important issues.

"Julian and Morton were early enemies and remained so until the end." according to Julian's daughter. This assessment was made of both men according to a tribute written in the *Indianapolis News* at the time of George Julian's death: "History looking at the lives of them both will probably say that Morton was more practical, and that Julian showed the finer idea, the purer purpose, the cleaner conception…In the death of George W. Julian, Indiana loses one of its most picturesque characters and society one of its finest forces."

Meredith and Julian had more extreme confrontations. Solomon Meredith ran against George Julian for Wayne County representative to Congress in 1864. Julian won and Meredith did not take his defeat well. In 1865, a battle of words commenced between Morton, Meredith and Julian over whether former slaves should have the vote and who should pay the war debt.

After a series of hot public speeches between Morton and Julian, Meredith took it upon himself to take care of Julian. A hulking, six-foot-four-inch-tall Meredith approached Julian in the Richmond railroad depot. Meredith struck Julian with either his fist or a metal bar, knocking him down. Julian could not defend himself because his arms were full of packages. Meredith began to beat Julian with a whip. When others tried to stop him, they were held back by several strong men who had come with Meredith.

Finally, the beating stopped, and Meredith left with his ruffians. Julian was picked up, bleeding and bruised, and taken to a doctor. Meredith was arrested and charged with assault. The charges were never brought to trial, and apparently Meredith was able to pull enough political strings to get off.

Levi Coffin

Levi Coffin (1798–1877) became known as a "conductor" on the Underground Railroad. He spent twenty years in Newport, Indiana. Levi and his family were denounced by Quakers who had different views about slavery. He was threatened by neighbors and slave hunters. At times, he suffered financial setbacks when people refused to do business with him. But through the fearful and discouraging times, Levi and his wife, Catherine, clung to their faith and determination to follow a path of sacrifice. They moved to Cincinnati to continue their work. After the Civil War, their efforts were amply rewarded by the love and esteem shown to them by the people they helped to reach freedom.

Levi Coffin spent many years traveling across the United States and in western Europe on behalf of the Freedman's Aid Commission. His mission was to raise funds to help escaped slaves and for other benevolent causes. After the Quakers' split over antislavery activity in the 1840s, the two separate Yearly Meetings merged again and became one.

The men mentioned previously and others who figured prominently in the history of Wayne County were well-regarded people of their times. There is no doubt about their strong convictions and their willingness to take on whatever challenges faced them. One can only look back with respect on lives well lived.

CONCLUSION

Residents of Wayne County are still fascinated with the battles for the courthouse. Newspaper stories and personal recollections abound, but many accounts are filled with conflicting details. Since 2003, I have looked into the facts, trying to get to the real story and the correct information.

Writing history about Wayne County gives one a new perspective on the people who raised their families, worked, played and worshiped here. They persevered through difficult times. They made plans and carried them out. Their religious faith and moral strength cannot be underrated.

Telling this story has been worth all of the effort of reading faded, handwritten documents, searching through old books and files and tiring out the eyes by reading microfilm. Truth can never hurt us, and history is not threatening. The challenge of today is to do as well or better than those who went before us.

BIBLIOGRAPHY

Books

Allison, Harold. *The Tragic Saga of the Indiana Indians*. Paducah, KY: Turner Publishing Company, 1986.

Brown, Samuel. *Western Gazette, or Emigrant's Directory*. Auburn, NY: H.C. Southwick, 1817.

Clark, Grace Julian. *George W. Julian*. Indianapolis: Indiana Historical Commission, 1923.

Cockrum, William M. *Pioneer History of Indiana*. Oakland City, IN: Press of Oakland City Journal, 1907.

Coffin, Levi. *Reminiscences*. Cincinnati, OH: Robert Clarke & Company, 1898.

The Dalbey brothers. *Dalbey's Souvenir Pictorial History of the City of Richmond, Indiana*. Richmond, IN: Nicholson Printing and Manufacturing, 1896.

Dana, Edmond. *Geographical Sketches on the Western Country Designed for Emigrants and Settler.* N.p.: General Books, LLC, 2010.

Dillon, John B. *History of Indiana, From Its Earliest Exploration by Europeans to the Close of the Territorial Government in 1816*. Indianapolis, IN: Bingham & Doughty, Publishers, 1959.

Dilts, Jon. *The Magnificent 92 Indiana Courthouses*. Bloomington, IN: Rose Bud Press Publishers, 1991.

Dunn, J.P., Jr. *Indiana: A Redemption From Slavery*. New York: Houghton Mifflin and Company, 1888.

Dunn, Jacob Piatt. *Indiana and Indianans: A History of Aboriginal and Territorial Indiana of the Century and Statehood*. New York: American Historical Society, 1919.

1884 Manufacturing and Mercantile of the Principal Places in Wayne, Henry, Delaware & Randolph Counties, Indiana. Knightstown, IN: Bookmark Reprint, 1978.

Emswiler, George P. *Poems and Sketches*. Richmond, IN: Nicholson Printing and Manufacturing, 1897.

Ewbank, Louis B., and Dorothy L. Riker, eds. *The Laws of Indiana Territory 1809–1816*. Indianapolis: Indiana Historical Bureau, 1934.

Feeger, Luther M. *A Brief History of Early Richmond*. Richmond, IN: Wayne County Historical Society, 1973.

Fisher, Richard S. *Indiana: In Relation to Its Geography, Statistics, Institutions, County Topography, Etc.* New York: J.H. Colton, 1854.

Fox, Henry Clay. *Memoirs of Wayne County and the City of Richmond.* Vols. 1 and 2. Madison, WI: Western Historical Association, 1912.

Harris, Branson L. *Some Recollections of My Boyhood*. Indianapolis, IN: Hollenbeck Press, 1908.

Hermansen, David R. *Indiana Courthouses of the Nineteenth Century*. Muncie, IN: Ball State University, 1968.

History of Wayne County, Indiana. Vols. 1 and 2. Chicago, IL: Inter-State Publishing Co., 1884.

Isaac, Norm. *Wayne-Ohio's Wilderness Warrior*. Dublin, IN: Prinit Press, 1982.

Jones, Daisy Marvel. *Richmond: Eastern Gateway to Indiana*. Richmond, IN: Richmond City Schools, 1954.

Knollenberg, Bernard. *Pioneer Sketches of the Upper Whitewater Valley, Quaker Stronghold of the West*. Indianapolis: Indiana Historical Society, 1949.

Lafever, Carolyn. *A Pictorial History of Wayne County, Indiana*. Virginia Beach, VA: Donning Company Publishers, 1998.

Lindley, Harlow, ed. *Indiana As Seen By Early Travelers: A Collection of Reprints from Books of Travel, Letters and Diaries Prior to 1830*. Indianapolis: Indiana Historical Commission, 1916.

Nelson, Paul David. *Anthony Wayne, Soldier of the Early Republic*. Bloomington: Indiana University Press, 1985.

Plummer, John T. *A Directory to City of Richmond, Together With a Historical Sketch*. Richmond, IN: R.O. Dormer & W.R. Holloway, Publishers, 1857. Palladium-Item Reprint, 1966.

Rabb, Kate Milner, ed. *A Tour Through Indiana in 1840: The Diary of John Parsons of Petersburg, Virginia*. New York: Robert M. McBride & Company, 1920.

Scott, John. *The Indiana Gazetteer, or Topographical Dictionary*. Centreville, IN: John Scott & Wm. M. Doughty, Publishers, 1826. Reprint, Indianapolis: Indiana Historical Society, 1954.

———. *Suggestive Plans for a Historical and Educational Celebration in Indiana in 1916*. Indianapolis: Indiana Centennial Celebration Committee, 1912.

Spahr, Walter E. *History of Centerville, Indiana*. Richmond, IN: Wayne County Historical Society, 1966.

Sylvester, Lorna Lutes. *"No Cheap Padding": Seventy-five Years of the Indiana Magazine of History, 1904–1979*. Indianapolis: Indiana Historical Bureau, 1980.

Territorial and State Acts and Journals of the General Legislature, 1811–1870. Indianapolis: Indiana State Archives.

Thornbrough, Gayle, and Dorothy Riker, eds. *Journals of the General Assembly of Indiana Territory 1805–1815*. Indianapolis: Indiana Historical Bureau, 1950.

Wasson, John M. (A Native). *Annals of Pioneer Settlers of the Whitewater and Its Tributaries in the Vicinity of Richmond, Ind. from 1804 to 1830*. Richmond, IN: Telegram Printing Company, 1875.

Wayne County Commissioners' Records, 1811–1835. Printed copy. Earlham College Library, Richmond, Indiana.

Wayne County Commissioners' Records, 1835–1875. Handwritten. Wayne County Commissioners' Office, Wayne County Courthouse, Richmond, Indiana.

Young, Andrew. *History of Wayne County, 1872*. Cincinnati, IN: Robert Clarke & Company, 1872.

MAGAZINE ARTICLES

Lafever, Carolyn. "The 'Last Sad Act.'" *Traces of Indiana and Midwest History* (Summer 1995). Found at Indianapolis, Indiana Historical Society.

MANUSCRIPTS, HOLDINGS AND UNPUBLISHED WORKS

Byron R. Lewis Historical Library, Vincennes University, Vincennes, Indiana.

Centerville Public Library. Microfilm and Document Collection. Centerville, Indiana.

Emswiler, George P. "First Villages." A talk for the Old Settlers' Picnic. Centerville, IN, 1897.

Indiana State Library. Newspaper Microfilm Collection. Indianapolis, Indiana.

Morrison-Reeves Library. Wayne County Newspaper Microfilm Collection. Richmond, Indiana.

Recchie, Nancy Ann. "Ohio Courthouses: An Inventory and an Analysis of Representative Nineteenth Century Architectural Styles." Thesis, University of Virginia, 1976.

Spahr, Walter. "History of Salisbury: The First County Seat." Thesis, Earlham College Library Archives, Richmond, Indiana.

Stiver, Inezetta, comp. Document collection, located at Historic Centerville and Centerville Public Library, Centerville, Indiana.

Wayne County Historical Museum. Documents and pictures. Richmond, Indiana.

Yount, Beverly, comp. Documents collection, located at Anderson Public Library, Anderson, Indiana.

ABOUT THE AUTHOR

Carolyn Ruth Lafever has been writing about the history of Wayne County and Hagerstown since 1982. She became a member of the board of trustees of the Hagerstown Museum and served as secretary and president. In 1986, she became the first director of the museum.

After leaving that position, Mrs. Lafever produced a video, *The Murals of Charles Newcomb*, for Historic Hagerstown. This led to the book of the same name, published in 1993. This interest in writing Wayne County history continued with the books *The Biggest Little Wild West Show on Earth, The Story of Buckskin Ben Stalker's Family Wild West Show*, *150 Years of the Wayne County Agricultural Fairs 1851–2001*, *Celebrate Our Schools* and *The Pictorial History of Wayne County*. Mrs. Lafever was a feature writer for local magazines *Senior Life*, *Lifestyles*, *Zeal* and *Maximum Living*. Her articles have appeared in several Indiana newspapers, *Antique Week* and the Indiana Historical Society magazine *Traces of Indiana and Midwestern History*.

Carolyn Lafever is a graduate of Ball State University with a master's degree in music and education. She and her husband Edward have four children and seven grandchildren. They live in rural Dalton Township near Hagerstown, Indiana.